W9-AZO-263

Forester

net ✓

$6 50
15¢

Reading the Woods

seeing
more
in
nature's
familiar
faces

Reading the Woods

Vinson Brown

STACKPOLE BOOKS

READING THE WOODS

Copyright © 1969 by
THE STACKPOLE COMPANY

Published by
STACKPOLE BOOKS
Cameron and Kelker Streets
Harrisburg, Pa. 17105

All rights reserved, including the right to reproduce this book or portions thereof in any form or by any means, electronic or mechanical, including photocopying, recording, or by any information storage and retrieval system, without permission in writing from the publisher. All inquiries should be addressed to Stackpole Books, Cameron and Kelker Streets, Harrisburg, Pennsylvania 17105.

To my daughter
TAMARA,
who shares with me my love for the wilderness
and deep woods, and to all kindred spirits.

Standard Book Number: 8117-1397-0
Library of Congress Catalog Card Number: 70-85652
Printed in U.S.A.

Contents

Influences on climate
•Glacial lakes •Mountains •Air masses
Climatic life zones
•Tropical •Lower Austral or Lower Sonoran •Upper Austral or Upper Sonoran •Transition •Canadian •Hudsonian •Arctic-Alpine
Telling about climate from nature's signs
•Tree rings •Plant spacing
The fascination of microclimates
•What shade does to plants •Shade and wildlife coloration •The roles of wind and fog

What wind does
•Steady winds •Storm winds •How trees ride out storms •How forests renew themselves after storms
Trees' built-in defenses against cold
•Leaf-shedding trees •Evergreens
The fearsome trio: sleet, ice, and snow
•Ice damage to tree cells •How snow protects trees from wind •Snow damage to tree limbs •Snow's boon to small animals: concealment from enemies
The blessing of gentle rain
How much rain a forest needs
•Sitka spruce forests of western Washington •Southern swamp forests •Redwood forests
Ruinous torrential rains

Acknowledgments

The maps on pp. 13, 14, and 33 are from the U.S. Department of Agriculture's *Yearbook of Agriculture 1941*. The chart on p. 14 is adapted from "Trees," *Yearbook of Agriculture 1949*, published by the U.S. Department of Agriculture and reproduced from *Sierra Nevadan Wildlife Region*, a Naturegraph book.

Illustrations on pp. 18, 20, 41, 85, and 91 are by Richard Wooster. Most of the marginal drawings in Chapters 7 and 8 are reproduced from William Carey Grimm, *The Book of Trees*, 1966 (The Stackpole Co.) and several Naturegraph books. Marginal pictures of beach pine, western larch, redwood, Monterey cypress, Sitka spruce, red huckleberry, and redwood sorrel are by Richard Wooster.

The author wishes to thank these organizations and individuals for furnishing the photographs on the following pages: U.S. Forest Service—pp. 5 (top), 27, 29 (top), 31 (bottom), 38, 39, 42, 43 (top), 47 (top), 54, 59 (bottom), 63, 74, 78 (bottom), 81, 84, 96, 98, 100, 101 (top), 105 (bottom), 107 (bottom), 110, 113 (bottom), 114, 117, 119, 120, 121, 124, 133, 139, 146, 150, 151; U.S. Department of Agriculture—pp. 15, 29 (bottom), 31 (top), 36 (top), 40, 50, 52 (top), 60 (bottom), 64, 66 (bottom), 68, 69, 70, 79 (bottom), 80 (top), 97, 105 (top), 111, 115, 122, 132; American Forests Products Industries, Inc.—pp. 21, 22, 49, 52 (bottom), 53, 59 (top), 61, 67, 80 (bottom), 83, 126, 138; Ontario Department of Lands and Forests—pp. 23, 36 (bottom), 55, 66 (top), 73 (top), 136 (top), 137; Alfred M. Bailey—pp. 25 (bottom), 113 (top), 116, 118 (insert); American Museum of Natural History—pp. 26, 35, 101 (bottom), 143; Cleveland Museum of Natural History—pp. 30, 136 (bottom), 145; Richard G. Beidlemen—p. 43 (bottom); Moulin Studios, San Francisco—p. 46; Library of Congress—pp. 47 (bottom), 79 (top), 82 (top), 95, 106; Canadian Wildlife Service—p. 60 (top); Michigan Department of Conservation—p. 62; Tennessee Department of Conservation—p. 73 (bottom); State of Illinois Department of Conservation—p. 134; National Park Service—pp. 77, 118; Southern Pacific—pp. 78 (top), 149, 152; Department of Forestry, University of California, Berkeley—p. 78 (center); Tennessee Valley Authority—pp. 82 (bottom), 107 (top); Eric M. Sanford, Alpha Photo Associates, New York, N.Y.—pp. 99, 130; Ontario Department of Natural Resources—p. 74; Redwood Empire Association—p. 125; Florida Board of Parks—p. 141; School of Forestry, University of Georgia—p. 142; and Paul Van Dyke—147.

Looking Behind
the Surface

STAND IN THE valley and look up to the hills. See the peaks covered with dark manes where the forests march, and see the gleam of water. There are stories there written by the ages—the slow change of the continents, drought that sears, rain that falls softly or roars in the flood, cold snaps and heat waves, snow on the passes... the hooves of the hunted and the claws of the killers, the drumbeat of woodpeckers, the march of plant diseases or insect hordes like invasions of Genghis Khan...the foolish destructiveness of man and the wisdom of his rebuilding, the crown fires that rage up the slopes and the slower-moving ground fires, the succession of plant life and its meaning, and the feel and spirit of the wilderness. Every step into the woods, or even to pass them slowly in a car, watching with seeing eyes, can be an adventure, a feeling of wonder, a joy in closeness to the out-of-doors when one understands what he sees behind nature's familiar faces.

The adventure lies in seeing deeper than the surface appearance of things and down to some of their inner meanings. The wonder lies in appreciating what one begins to understand and savoring it in the mind and heart in a way that makes a person feel one with all living things and even the rocks and the hills. The learner becomes aware how different the forest is in the moonlight from in the daylight and what it is saying to him on the night breezes, and how the darkness the clouds bring changes the feeling of the day even as the brightness of the sun. When a person who knows the outdoors sees the shape of a leaf, it tells him a story of the climate, the movement of life down the ages, and the balance of shade and light. He sees roots exposed and looks around the forest to see the causes and, because he has learned to read the woods, he looks into the future too and knows what can happen that may bring disaster and what could happen that would be a victory.

So the woods become to the initiate a moving story, a movement of centuries, a movement of leaves and the life that flies and runs and climbs among them, a movement of waters through the leaf mold and the soil, a constant movement of growth and struggle, of the fight of the treetops for sunlight or the struggle of the roots for water and minerals. One sees after awhile the movement of whole forests and the movement of what is called plant succession, when one kind of plant life takes the place of another as conditions change. And all this and much more is written before a person's eyes if he will seek to read and to understand.

HOW TO USE THIS BOOK

The chapters and topics given in the table of contents of this book are your first key to using the book to read the woods. They set the focus of your eyes so that you begin to see not just a mass of trees, but variations and details that have meanings. Chapters 1 through 5 tell about signs to read in the woods, and Chapters 6 through 8 describe our wealth of plant communities.

We read advertising signs along the road and other communications humans make with letters and pictures. As we ride or drive or walk through a woods, we are constantly seeing other signs but many of us do not understand them. There is a richness of the mind and the spirit that a person can gain from learning to read these hidden signs. As one learns how climate and weather change and influence the woods, also how animals, birds, insects, fire, man, and other influences are all shaping, building, destroying, moving and changing plants; how even the earth and the leaf mold that form a cushion under one's feet tell fascinating stories, he comes to feel himself a part of the great circle of earth and sky and all life, knowing it with some of that keen understanding and sensitivity the Indian of America had in the long ago.

The signs given in this book are mainly the most common, but once they start to open your eyes to look carefully and to understand, they will make you aware of many other signs of what the woods are saying, and you will have the ground training needed to begin to understand these other signs too. For those more deeply interested, informative books are listed in the Suggested References.

In Chapters 6 through 8, as you learn about the great plant communities, such as the redwood forest of the Pacific Northwest, or the longleaf, loblolly, and shortleaf pine barrens and savannas of the southeastern states, familiarize yourself with the common species of each by studying the brief descriptions and the drawings of leaves and fruits or nuts. Soon you begin to realize each of these communities is like a kingdom, ruled by characteristic monarchs made of wood and bark and leaf, each often distinctive in feeling, sound, smell, and sight. A man who could read the woods could probably walk blindfolded in many of them and tell where he was merely by touch of bark, smell of leaf, the different sounds of the wind whispering in the foliage, and the crackle of his clothes brushing the undergrowth.

Read about the plant communities near you first, and then those farther away so that at last you will feel each a familiar part of the living earth, a place to be loved and visited with reverence and joy as one might come back after a long journey to a beloved home. Thus is this book twofold in its purpose: first to make you aware, from a perusal of the first half of the book, of some of the little signs that call from every passing vista as you walk or ride in our woods, and then to enable you to weave them with understanding mind, through information contained in the last half of the book, into the greater majesty of whole forests and the vast waves of greenery that roll over the distant hills.

Indeed, should not more and more people learn the enchantment and riches of our woods? Man cannot desert the green heart of the world and wander in the cities of stone and steel without becoming in time a lost being, who needs more than anything else, though he may understand it not, the peace and spirit of those dim and glowing worlds where the vines hang down from clustered branches and the leaves make sighing talk against the sky.

CHAPTER ONE

Recognizing How Climates Make Woods

ODAY ENORMOUS GLACIERS of ice inch their way over the vast island of Greenland in the Far North. But ten thousand years ago similar glaciers groaned and thundered across Minnesota and down the California Sierras, reached a long arm into the Appalachians, and rolled boulders down the slopes of the Colorado Rockies. That great ice age leaves its mark yet on our own climates and weather, for those billions of tons of white cold tore out of the ground of our continent the holes for twenty thousand lakes, from the tiny ones of some alpine meadows among the peaks of the Rockies to the great inland seas we call the Great Lakes.

INFLUENCES ON CLIMATE

Glacial Lakes

Now the mist and other moisture rise out of glacial lake waters and spread their influence over the lands, watering the forests of the present because of the ice mountains of the past and storing the water needed to feed the roots of many forests. Twice, three times, four times and maybe more the almost equally great lakes of our intermountain west have grown and then retreated again in endless warfare with the deserts since the southernmost glaciers died. Great Salt Lake today stands in Utah as a monument and reminder of a far greater lake that once covered today's thousands of square miles of sand flat, salt brush, and sage, and tells of days when forests lined its banks and the climate was far more moist.

Mountains

Mountains also have a considerable bearing on our climatic regions. The Appalachians and Adirondacks of the East are like worn-down teeth, very ancient mountains, sandpapered by the rains and winds and ice and snow of more than a million centuries, their influence on the weather blunted by age so that the differences of climate east and west of these ranges are only mild. This is particularly so since moisture from the Atlantic Ocean, the Gulf of Mexico, and the Great Lakes flows north and south and west into all the eastern half of the United States and Canada.

On the other hand, the youthful Sierras, Rockies, and Cascades still thrust their peaks skyward high enough to create vast pockets of dryness to the east of their ranges where deserts and semideserts reign. Even the California Coast Range is high enough to seal off much of the Great Valley of California into semidesert dryness, though high winds carry clouds of moisture across the valley to deposit their moisture as snow on the middle slopes of the Sierras. This explains the lush "snow forests" of red fir on the middle slopes of the mountains.

Air Masses

All of North America is influenced in climate by what are called air masses, vast stretches of thousands of cubic miles of similar type air that move in cyclic and often predictable ways across land and sea. Each such air mass is apparently the creature of the area in which it is born. Thus the polar Canadian air mass brings its cold, dry air out of the inland heart of northern Canada and moves southward in winter to be moisturized by the Great Lakes, where snowstorms often bring greater moisture to the land near them than reaches the land farther north or south or west.

The tropical Gulf or tropical Atlantic air mass is warm and moist, bringing the typical muggy summer days of the eastern and midwestern states as it moves north in summer. By contrast, a deep sea smell and a cold and blustering wind, followed by rain or snow, usually comes down from the northern Atlantic to the northeast states in the form of the polar Atlantic air mass.

Polar Pacific is cool and moist because it is made in the vast reaches of the North Pacific and moves southward in winter to break the typical Pacific Coast summer drought and bring rain from Washington to California. Tropical Pacific is much drier and warmer, coming up from the south in summer with the typical balmy, dry, sunny days of California. Sometimes it even comes north in winter, bringing hot sunny days to California in January and explaining the light plant cover of the southern half of that state. Out of the hot, dry heart of Mexico comes the tropical continental air mass, riding its rainless winds into the deserts and semideserts of the American West that it has produced.

CLIMATIC LIFE ZONES

Wherever these great air masses meet each other there is usually warfare, especially where a dry air mass like polar Canadian meets a wet air mass like tropical Gulf. Dark clouds pile into the sky, winds rage, and rain falls till the land may be flooded, all of this telling of the battle of the giants! The cyclical and regular movement of these air masses, mainly from north to south, channeled by mountain ranges and seacoasts, and influenced by bodies of water such as the Great Lakes, is constantly triggered by the advance and retreat of the sun north and south over the continent

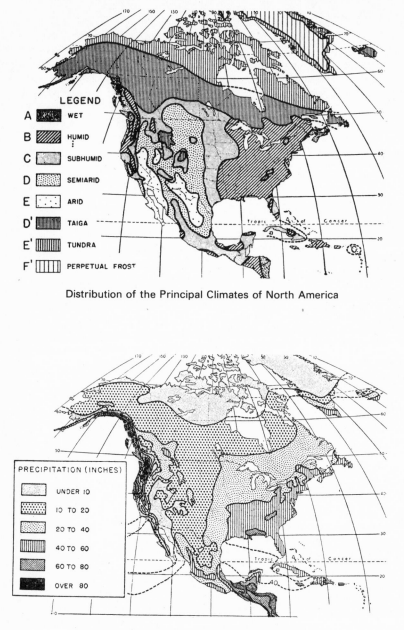

LEGEND

A — WET
B — HUMID
C — SUBHUMID
D — SEMIARID
E — ARID
D' — TAIGA
E' — TUNDRA
F' — PERPETUAL FROST

Distribution of the Principal Climates of North America

PRECIPITATION (INCHES)

UNDER 10
10 TO 20
20 TO 40
40 TO 60
60 TO 80
OVER 80

Distribution of Precipitation Over North America

from winter to summer. The results create typical weather patterns throughout the year over vast areas, which we call climatic zones and where the types of forests and woods that prevail reflect the climates that have created them. The first two maps in this chapter show the principal climates of North America and also the variations in precipitation for different areas. Notice how these two maps tie in together in a general way and also are reflected in the vegetation types shown in the third map. Thus denser

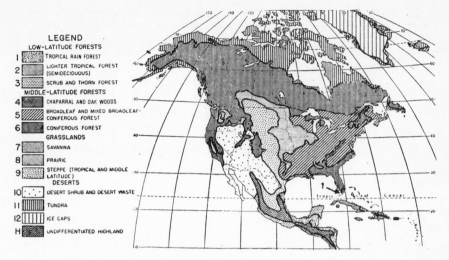

LEGEND

LOW-LATITUDE FORESTS

1 TROPICAL RAIN FOREST

2 LIGHTER TROPICAL FOREST (SEMIDECIDUOUS)

3 SCRUB AND THORN FOREST

MIDDLE-LATITUDE FORESTS

4 CHAPARRAL AND OAK WOODS

5 BROADLEAF AND MIXED BROADLEAF-CONIFEROUS FOREST

6 CONIFEROUS FOREST

GRASSLANDS

7 SAVANNA

8 PRAIRIE

9 STEPPE (TROPICAL AND MIDDLE LATITUDE)

DESERTS

10 DESERT SHRUB AND DESERT WASTE

11 TUNDRA

12 ICE CAPS

H UNDIFFERENTIATED HIGHLAND

Distribution of the Principal Vegetative Formations in North America

forests are found in the more humid areas. However, the coniferous forests of the southeastern United States reflect a very much warmer climate than the similar coniferous forests of the northern states and Canada.

Biologists have developed the idea of climatic life zones mainly on the basis of different plants that grow at different latitudes and different elevations, as influenced by differences in average temperatures and also by quantities of rainfall or snowfall. Typical animals are also found in these different zones so that the whole concept is

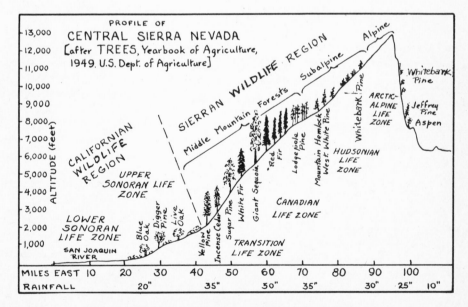

Climatic Life Zones of the Central Sierra Nevada Mountains

useful in recognizing the influence of climatic zones on animal and plant life. These living things thus act as signposts as you travel north and south or travel up and down a high mountainside.

Starting from the far south we have (1) the tropical zone, where jungle trees are prevalent (this zone is found in the United States only in southern Florida and in Hawaii), (2) the Lower Austral or Lower Sonoran zone, where semi-tropical swamps and pine savannas are found in the southeastern states and the cactus and creosote scrub deserts are found in the West, as well as the dry grassland of California's Great Valley, (3) the Upper Austral or Upper Sonoran zone, where mainly deciduous forests or pine savannas are found in the East and Midwest, while dry chaparral scrub wood-lands, oak woods and sagebrush deserts are found in the West, (4) the transition zone, where mixed coniferous-hardwood forests are found in the East and Midwest, while mixed oak and Douglas fir forests, redwoods, and ponderosa pine forests are the typical plant communities of this zone found in the West, (5) the Canadian zone, where solid coniferous forests of the true firs, spruces, hemlocks, and larches are the rule, (6) the Hudsonian zone, where alpine fir, alpine larch, and various specialized high-altitude pines, such as the whitebark pine, struggle to exist in a bleak windy environment on the edge of eternal cold, and (7) the Arctic-Alpine zone, where trees cannot live, but only quick-growing grasses, sedges, and small herbs that spring up in the brief summer of the Far North or the high mountaintops.

The cross-section diagram of the Sierras shows how these zones extend up and down the slopes of these mountains, and what are the typical trees to be found in each zone. These are some of the signs talking to you as you ride or walk through the woods.

TELLING ABOUT CLIMATE FROM NATURE'S SIGNS

Tree Rings

The tree rings shown in the accompanying photograph are another of such signs in the woods, for they show how the climate has changed through the years in the

Cross section of tree, showing rings that tell us stories about the years of the tree's life and its age.—*Photo courtesy U.S. Department of Agriculture.*

area where the tree lives. You can find these signs in a stump, or in a tree just cut down to be taken away by the lumberman. Where a ring is very narrow it shows a year of little moisture so that the tree did not have much help in its growth. Where the rings are wide, you are told the year was a good year for this tree with much moisture and sun to help it grow. A tree may often show clusters of narrow rings and other clusters of wide rings, showing that years of drought usually came in cycles or bunches as also did good years of moisture and growth.

Narrow rings on one side of a tree and wide rings on the other may show that cold, fierce winds have stunted growth on the windward side, while the protected side has grown more regularly. Sometimes you can even project these rings into the future and prophesy not only the future of the tree but the future of local yearly weather. Thus, if the last several rings on the tree are narrow ones, but there were several before that were wide, you can predict that soon good, moist years will be coming for the tree and the locality. Of course, this can also mean the coming of great storms that produce floods and erosion.

Plant Spacing

There are many other signs to watch for that tell us about the effects of climate. For example, many ferns, much moss, and many large-leaved vines in the undergrowth of a forest are a sign of heavy rainfall in the area. Widely spaced trees with few shrubs below them tell us that here the rainfall is probably rather low or between 15 and 30 inches a year. Still more widely spaced desert trees with numerous spines, such as the saguaro cacti and the Joshua trees in the southwest deserts (see Desert Woodlands under Deciduous Forests of the West in Chapter 8), tell us of extreme desert conditions with rainfall usually well below 10 inches a year.

THE FASCINATION OF MICROCLIMATES

Our ranch house is on a south-facing slope, well touched by the sun in both winter and summer. So even our winters are comparatively balmy, with the frost rarely reaching below the outer skin of the ground, or an inch or so at most. But hardly a quarter of a mile up in the hills behind us stands another house that lies at the beginning of a dark canyon. In the winter the chill of the canyon comes down to that house and icy fingers of winter may reach even a foot underground, freezing the pipes of the people and cutting off their water supply for days. Thus are two very different microclimates (miniature climates) found within only a few hundred yards of each other! Here we can grow lemon and orange trees. There they can grow apples and peaches, but no citrus trees at all.

If you move through the woods, especially in hilly country, you may see signs of different microclimates all around, and it is fun to learn to read their signs. Microclimates are caused by many things, including various kinds of shade, exposure to sunlight, exposure to winds, fog, salt air of the sea, wide temperature variations, the influence of nearby bodies of water, hot springs, man-made temperatures or fumes, and so forth. They may also be caused by rock and soil. Dark soil and rock attract heat and so hold it longer in an area at night; light soil and rock reflect heat and so increase the cold at night.

What Shade Does to Plants

In the night's darkness most plants rest and are quiet unless the wind is rustling through their leaves. But in the daytime all are seeking minerals, water, and sunlight, for all three are combined to be turned into new plant cells for the storage of food. Thus, one might think of shade as being an enemy of plants because it takes away from them the sunlight they need. If this were true, then most plants would be out in sunny places, soaking up the life-giving sun. But, actually, plants are often thickest where there is shade, though we do notice that where there is too much shade, as in the California redwoods, there is not much undergrowth.

Thus we can state as a rule of thumb that, assuming similar soil conditions, plants increase in number up to what appears to be a certain optimum condition of sun and shade in combination, but, above and below this point, more shade or more sun, or less shade or less sun, seems to decrease the thickness of plant growth. Why is this so? It is because too much sun sucks up too much water from trees and other plants, cutting down the effectiveness of growth, while too much shade may allow too little sunlight to reach through and give the plants the help in growth they need. A certain amount of shade is needed to help most young trees start growing, but too much may prevent their growth. The actual amount may greatly vary. Thus young lodgepole pines and quaking aspens need practically no shade at all for beginning growth, while hemlocks and most firs in their youth demand considerable shade. Often you may see in the woods a group of young trees that have sprung up where a giant old tree has recently fallen to let down some sunlight, but in many thick, dark forests young trees of most of the species that are growing there may not be able to get a start because of the shade.

Where fire has burned or man cleared an opening in the forest, new plants begin to spring up soon after the destruction. Each tells its own story in certain signs. The grass and small-leaved herbs that spring up first tell us of plants that love lots of sunlight, for their narrow leaves are created to preserve them from having the moisture they contain dried up by the sun. Often such leaves are tough to the feel and even coated sometimes with a kind of shellaclike material that keeps them from giving off too much moisture. But these swift-growing plants soon give enough shade to protect the growth of young bushes. The slow-growing bushes begin to drown out the grass and herbs with shade as they rise above them, protecting the soil with greater shade and dropping leaves and twigs on it to increase its organic content so it gradually becomes moist and thick enough for young fast-growing trees, like the aspen in the West and the jack pine in the Midwest. These trees finally give shade for the seedling trees of the real forest giants, such as the pines, spruces, and firs. As these slowly rise in majesty over their lesser cousins, they produce so much shade that the earlier but smaller trees are finally drowned out in too heavy shade and die. In their place there grow up herbs and bushes with large leaves especially adapted for living under the shade of the big trees and finding bits of sunlight that sift down through the foliage. Thus is the wonderful circle of shade building on shade completed. (For further discussion of plant succession, see Chapter 6 and the heading Nurse Trees in Chapter 4.)

Notice in the following picture how the size of the leaves of the plants shows their relation to shade so that you can often read at a glance just how much shade-loving or sun-loving a particular plant may be. Thus the sun-loving plants of sunny south-facing slopes usually have small leaves so that they will not lose too much moisture from the sun, while the shade-loving plants of dark north-facing slopes or under the canopy of a thick forest, usually have large leaves for catching sunlight. All the gradations in between help teach you the signs of each plant's reaction to its need for sunlight and shade.

When flying over any wooded hilly or mountainous area in an airplane you will soon notice, if you keep your eyes alert for the signs of the woods, that the direction of the hill slopes has a great effect on the types of plants that grow on them. The south-

Influence of Shade in Forest on Leaves

a. Live oak trees of streamside woodland in California are highest trees of this forest, so get more sunlight and have smaller leaves. b. White alders underneath in second story of forest have somewhat larger leaves because of shadier position and need for larger leaves to get more sunlight. c. Thimbleberry in third story of forest has still larger leaves because of still more shade. d. Trillium is in bottom story of forest where there is most shade and least sunlight so leaves are largest of all (though, because of space limitations, they do not appear so here).

Influence of Slope Direction on Plants

Plants on left in this picture are trees because this north-facing slope gives more shade for growth and protection from sun in warm climate (such as lower slopes of Colorado Rockies). Plants on right are bushes adapted to high summer heat and much sunlight; they have mainly smaller and more leathery leaves because they are on a south-facing slope.

facing slopes, especially their highest parts, are generally much lighter-colored than the north-facing slopes, while the deep canyons and their steep north-facing slopes usually appear very dark green. (This is shown dramatically in the photo of Red River Canyon under Middle-Altitude Rocky Mountain Forests in Chapter 7.) This darkness or lightness of the green color of the leaves is due mainly to the fact that the magic green cells, or chlorophyll, that create food out of water, sunlight, and minerals, have to work harder in shade-shielded places than where the sunlight is easily received. Thus the green chlorophyll cells are closer together in and thicker in the leaves on the shady slopes, making these leaves generally darker green. There are exceptions to this rule, as some plants of the chaparral in California, almost all sun-loving plants, have darker green leaves. An example is the pea chaparral. It will be noticed also that leaves in shady places are often arranged in beautifully symmetrical tiers in order for each leaf to get the maximum amount of sunlight possible. This is not necessary in the more sunny areas. Thus do the slopes of the hills produce several different micro-climates in which leaf color, leaf distribution, and leaf size and shape all help you read the signs that tell the meaning of each plant's place in nature.

Examine the accompanying picture which shows how plant growth is affected by the special effects of shade and light that hit the area in which the plants live.

Shade and Wildlife Coloration

Animals and birds also give us signs by their colors and shades of color how they are adapted to live in each of these microclimates. Thus the dark blue and black Steller's jay loves the shade of the darker forests of the West, while the lighter blue and gray scrub jay of California, Arizona, and Florida is a bird of the open scrub forests of oak and chaparral where the sunlight not only makes the leaves lighter, but the brighter, lighter colors of rock and soil are more plainly visible. So also do we find that field mice found in meadows where there is much sunlight always appear lighter in color than similar-appearing but darker-skinned mice of the nearby forest.

This great variation in color and shade and in size and shape of leaves allows us not only to read the woods like a book, but to sense a mood and feeling to each plant community and the patterns of life within it that make a mosaic of beauty and wonder. In the more open sunny areas we hear more frequently the joy of birdsong, the trill of crickets or locusts, and the scurrying of small feet through the grass, making these places regions of laughter and music in which a thousand light colors and shades, often shifted by the wind in the leaves, dance before us. But in the dark shadows of the great coniferous forests a silence falls, in which even the note of a thrush high in the tree-tops is only a muted echo, emphasizing the quiet. Here, if our hearts are open, we may sense a peace and reverence for soft dark beauty that brings us close to the spirit of the wild. A beam of light, one only out of many that have sought their way down through the jungle of leaves above us, may strike a woods violet at our feet and bring out the delicate mauve and purple beauty of its petals till our own beings glow with the same magic.

The Roles of Wind and Fog

Wind is a carver of the shapes of trees and sometimes even a destroyer of trees and shrubs, but its power to shape or destroy is often determined by the walls that the rocks of hills, cliffs, and mountains form. These walls along our coasts also determine where the land clouds we call fog may be allowed to wander and help the growth of plants, especially by giving them dampness during the heat of summer. Thus we can often tell by signs plants give us whether they have been helped, hindered, or shaped by wind or fog.

· The redwood forest, shown under Pacific Coastal Coniferous Forests in Chapter 7, is the perfect example of a forest nurtured by fog during summer's heat. Where the canyons of the California coast allow this fog to creep inland the great trees flourish, but, wherever walls of rocks stop this progress of the dampness from the sea, the redwood trees stop growing as if cut off by a giant hand. So the very presence of these trees tells us of frequent and thick fogs without ever having to see those fogs, and so also do other plants associated with the redwoods (see illustrated chart). But where winds are too strong redwoods and many other trees cannot grow because their shallow root systems cannot stand the strike of the great storm winds. Thus, close to the sea, the redwoods do not grow, but the closed-cone pine trees and the cypresses grow because they have deep tap roots that hold against the gales. Fortunately fogs can go around corners that winds cannot, and so reach the redwoods far inland up the valleys and canyons. So the redwoods speak of quiet peace and hissing fog, while the pines and cypresses of the coast tell us of the scream of the great winds, and their shapes are twisted to tell us the story.

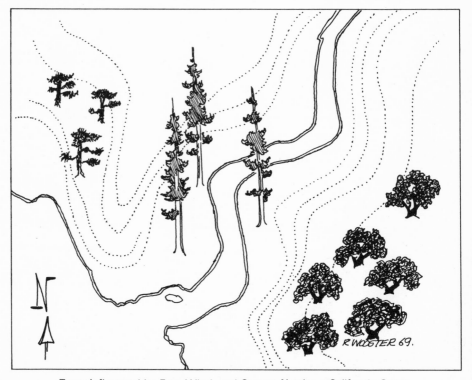

Trees Influenced by Fog, Wind, and Sun on Northern California Coast

Trees at upper left are beach pines, stunted and warped by wind, but holding to their places by strong roots. Trees in center are redwoods in valley sheltered from strong winds by hills which allow fog to reach them and supply needed moisture in summer. Trees at bottom right are live oak trees on hillside too high for heavy fog, and with good afternoon sun exposure.

CHAPTER TWO

Seeing the Tales of Weather

THE LONG, STEADY, dry winds of the Great Plains, drying up the ground and sweeping a thousand miles or more over mainly flat country, make tree life very difficult. Hence the wide vistas of the grasslands. The cottonwoods and willows grow mainly where the rivers have cut deep troughs below the sweep of the wind and where there is enough moisture. At the western end of the plains the cedar breaks on the hills, as they are called, are really clumps of gnarled, knotty, deep-rooted juniper trees and a few pinyon pines, that bow and fight but live before the most savage winds, clinging to both ridgetop and canyon rim (see Intermountain Pinyon-Juniper Woodlands in Chapter 7).

Windswept mature balsam fir near Parson's Pond, Newfoundland.—*Photo courtesy American Forest Products Industries, Inc.*

WHAT WIND DOES

Steady Winds

The great steady winds of the ocean shore and the mountaintops and plains roll in seldom ceasing pressure against the deep-rooted wind-fighters, who give before them and stream out like tattered flags in the direction the wind rules them (see photo on p. 21). The very force of this steady wind can be gauged approximately by the degree of angle to which a tree is bent. Thus a complete right-angle turn in the wind direction by a tree means it has very likely been subject for long times during its life to winds approaching fifty miles an hour or more (called "a whole gale" by weather experts). Only such terrific winds can so completely reshape the direction of a tree. A forty-mile-an-hour steady wind (called "a gale") may possibly bend a tree about two-thirds of the distance to the right angle. These approximations suggest a scientific project for the reader: take a wind-bent tree, measure its angle, and then determine with a good wind gauge the actual force of the wind striking this tree on the average over a year's time.

Storm Winds

Winds of more than fifty-five miles an hour, called whole gales (55-63), storms (64-75), and hurricanes (75 miles an hour and up), are the tree reapers and destroyers, as also are the tornadoes that whirl at still higher speeds when they strike. The signs of a tornado are easily recognized in any forest because the trees have been lifted, torn, and tossed about in a clearly seen whirling position; even their trunks and branches are often twisted unnaturally. The other storms may have terrible gusts of great power, but their strength is felt like the ripping swipe of the paw of an enraged grizzly bear, traveling in one direction.

Forester surveys timber knocked down or injured by Hurricane Donna in Florida. An estimated 150 trees per acre were snapped by the fierce winds.—*Photo courtesy American Forests Products Industries, Inc.*

Regeneration among wind-damaged trees, Sudbury District, Ontario, Canada.—*Photo courtesy Ontario Department of Lands and Forests.*

HOW TREES RIDE OUT STORMS   Hurricanes hit the Atlantic and Gulf coasts of the United States and leave wide swaths of fallen trees in the forests and woods where they strike. The power of the strike can be gauged by the size of the trees that have been knocked down and the smashed appearance of the branches (see photo). If you come on such a place, imagine for a moment yourself in that forest when that great wind powered into it and be thankful you were not there, for your chances of living would have been very small! But notice that, though about 150 trees per acre were snapped in two or crushed by the hurricane in the picture, still many trees were left standing. This may be a sign not so much of strength as resilience. Such trees bowed before the wind and did not snap, very much as grass stems bow before great winds and straighten themselves when the winds have passed.

A close examination of such trees struck by a hurricane should show us some interesting things. Trees with weaknesses caused by disease, or insect or animal damage, would probably be among the first to go down, but also certain species of trees would fall or break easier than others. Trees with deep tap roots, like the oaks, should hold against the storm fairly well, except that oak wood is comparatively brittle and therefore might snap. Hickories should certainly stand up well because they have about the toughest wood known, but ashes should do well because of their resiliency. Cottonwoods, having weak wood, should break easily, but their seeds would bring them back in the form of young trees rather quickly in such a devastated area.

HOW FORESTS RENEW THEMSELVES AFTER STORMS   The accompanying photograph shows a forest of hemlocks, spruces, beeches, maples, and balsam fir that had been struck by a great storm, but were recuperating from their ordeal. It is evident that some of the taller trees were so stripped of their bark by the wind that they died even though they were not knocked down or broken. So a tough bark is important in resisting wind just as is a tough wood. However, life rebuilds where even terrible storms have destroyed, and the young firs and spruces can be seen growing up again to replace the dead trees of the past. In fact, some young trees grow up more rapidly and easily because of the presence of the dead, whose leaves are soon gone and so allow the sunlight to give strength and life to the new generation.

Man may help with such restoration of life when he comes in and cleans out the dead trees or cuts them up to form a mulch that will re-create the fine soil as decay breaks up the parts further. So, out of the earth and the death of the old, killed by the wind, new life finds a way to remake the destroyed world.

TREES' BUILT-IN DEFENSES AGAINST COLD

Leaf-shedding Trees

Man has to worry about cold when winter comes—ice on the road, frozen pipes, snow too deep for cars, blizzards that blind the eyes of drivers. Trees withdraw their life forces inward when the great cold comes, much as men try to retreat into warm houses. The sap if it rose in winter would freeze, expand, and probably burst and kill the life in the cambium just beneath the bark. So the deciduous trees save their lives through the wonderful process of shedding their leaves, at the same time putting on a display of glorious color. With the leaves gone, the sap can no longer be pulled up the threads of life beneath the bark.

Evergreens

The conifers, clothed in their dark green needles, disdainfully seem to rise above this fear of death from cold, but even they have ways to hold back the running of the surface sap, and the needles, protected by being partly of wood and covered with a coat of resin, go into some kind of sleep in which the green chlorophyll is no longer active at creating food and so in need of mineralized water from the soil.

THE FEARSOME TRIO: SLEET, ICE, AND SNOW

Even though they prepare themselves each fall for the coming of cold, both co-nifers and deciduous trees, such as the maples and oaks, cannot always meet every crisis that may befall them. Often in the following spring and summer we may still see the effects of the disasters that hit certain trees amidst storm or freezing cold, for most such events leave their signs.

The birches, hard maples, white ashes, and elms that stand so forlornly under the icy clothing left by a sleet storm (see photo) have suffered damages, some so severe that an early death will be the only answer. If you see trees dark with death, also live trees with large limbs snapped off and dead branches the next summer, you will be able to guess what has happened. The ice that clings may break off twigs or even branches, and its cold may bite through the cambium, breaking the precious cells that carry moisture. When too many cells die, the tree also begins to die as a man dies who is frozen in a blizzard.

Up on the mountaintops snow, if not too heavily weighted by water, may actually

Northern hardwood stand of birch, hard maple, elm, and white ash frozen in ice after severe sleet storm.—*Photo courtesy U.S. Forest Service.*

be a protector for trees during the winter of howling winds. See the picture of Engelmann spruces in the high Rockies that have been exposed above the snow by the wind and so pressed down by it. The part of a tree under the snow in such places may show comparatively normal growth. Often the tree parts above snow in such localities may be killed by drying out and great cold, thus stunting their growth to snow height from year to year (see also Subalpine Forests under Coniferous Forests of the West in Chapter 7). In a hollow, where the snow lies deep, but at the same altitude, the tree may reach much greater height because of greater protection. However, if the snow is too wet and heavy, it can break limbs in such places, and signs of this we should also watch for.

Down in the lower country of the northern states and Canada an unusually wet and heavy snow (as shown in the picture) may strip a tree of some of its outer and especially its longer branches by weighting them down until they snap. Snow of any kind protects many of the smaller animals of the forest, such as the mice and shrews, not only from cold but also from fierce enemies like the weasels, owls, and hawks, who

Sprawling Engelmann spruces at 12,000 feet altitude near Berthoud Pass, Colorado. Good examples of timberline trees.—*Photo by Alfred M. Bailey.*

Wet and heavy snow on trees.—*Photo courtesy American Museum of Natural History.*

cannot find the little creatures where they burrow in their small tunnels along the ground beneath the drifts. As the snow melts in the spring, these tunnels appear first through the wasting drifts as dark streaks and then as either little furrows where a myriad tiny feet have run and worn or pressed down the soil, or as small ridges where mice, shrews, or moles have burrowed slightly below the surface of the ground, pushing up the soil. About them the many broken long branches and many twigs, piling much trash on the forest floor, give us a sign that tells us some very deep and wet snow fell here on some winter days.

RAIN

The Blessing of Gentle Rain

Water, sun, and minerals are the great creators of plant life, but water, mainly in the form of rain, shows us the most spectacular variations and results. Rain, the good mother, and sister of the Earth mother, as some Indians called her, comes best as a long gentle fall that soaks gradually into the leaf mold and the ground, building up the hidden water supplies of the hills and the valleys so that the trees may drink deeply and grow mightily, as the thick rings of a good rain year show (see Telling about Climate from Nature's Signs in Chapter 1). Rain sets up the mightiest forests of our continent, the rain forests of the Pacific Coast, with redwoods, Douglas firs, and Sitka spruces as the dominant trees. In these forests the trees are so thick that few rays of the sun reach the ground and the leaf mold is so rich that your foot sinks into it as into a Persian rug of great value.

How Much Rain a Forest Needs

Reading the signs of the woods, we can look at many a wood or forest and guess closely the rainfall that has made it appear as it does. The dense Sitka spruce forests

Timber killed by flood residue in Mt. Rainier National Park in Washington. A total loss of trees!—*Photo courtesy U.S. Forest Service.*

of western Washington are true rain forests with well over 100 inches of rain a year. The swamp forests of the southern states reach their rank growth with 50 to 75 inches of rain a year, but with much humidity to help and rain evenly spaced throughout the year. The redwood forests also grow thickly, but with much less undergrowth, on from 35 to 90 inches of rain per year, though depending on heavy fogs in the summertime to keep them from drying out. Oftentimes poor, or worn-out soil, keeps growth down even when the rainfall is good. The widely spaced pine savannas in the southern and southeastern states (see Southern and Southeastern Pine and Oak-Pine Woods in Chapter 7) are an example of this, as the rainfall here ranges from about 40 to 50 inches per year. Thus appearances can be deceiving, and all factors need to be accounted for.

Ruinous Torrential Rain

Someday you may come on a part of a forest that looks as if it has been killed by fire until a closer look reveals that there is no sign of burning. Thinking that insects or diseases have killed these trees, you look still closer and see no sign of this work either (see Harmful Insects in Chapter 5). Now you should look at the ground beneath the trees and find the signs of the work of water, coming not as a good and kind mother, but as a death-bringing demon. The sign is the heavy gravel and silt standing high around the bases of the dead trunks (see photo), telling of rain coming in torrents, falling from the sky as in the days of Noah, until a flood has penetrated the forest, cutting air off from its roots for too long and killing it. It is a death that man too often has a hand in, as we shall learn later (see Man's Wasteful Practices in Chapter 5).

CHAPTER THREE

Knowing the Story in the Soil

MOTHER EARTH IS truly like a woman. She trembles and shakes in the form of earthquakes, snaps back angrily in the form of land- and snowslides, but gives the milk of her love in the form of mineralized water to all growing plants. Out of her rise the leafy heads of woods and great forests, to tower far above her in their pride, but, without her, they would be nothing, for it is her skin, the soil, that gives them life and sustenance. This skin of the earth is endlessly forming, like our own skin, some daily being destroyed, but some always being added to and renewed. It is mainly man, the great enemy of himself and of all life, who, too often, upsets the balance by causing that life-giving skin, the soil, to be stripped away too fast by the action of bulldozers, saws, and other mechanized gadgets that man plays with like a child with its toys, without realizing the damage they can do.

The kind of skin or soil any part of the earth has can be read by the signs of the woods and forests that grow out of it (or their lack of growth if the soil is wrong for them), and we see the signs of the movements of soils, sands, and rocks and their destruction in the ways plants have reacted to these movements or the destruction. Thus, all around us the woods are talking about the earth and all its changes with their unconscious sign language. Though they, of course, are not trying to communicate with us, yet the signs they give us have both warning and promise, and the seeds of happiness as well as despair.

Early stage of soil formation, showing lichens, mosses, and small ferns on boulder.—
Photo courtesy U.S. Forest Service.

SOIL IN THE MAKING

How Tiny Lichens Crack Great Rocks

If you walk in the woods and come to some great rock or boulder left there long ago by a mighty glacier or the vast movement of waters, you are likely to see the beginning of Mother Earth's skin, the soil at its dawning. The accompanying picture shows a great boulder, covered with tiny lichens (plants that are a partnership of both an alga and a fungus), mosses, and small ferns. Most of the lichens are like flat maps against the rocks and are of many colors, being the first of all plants to start growing on a plain rock surface. A few kinds of lichens form almost leaflike growths. Lichens produce an acid that acts upon the rocks, gradually creating tiny cracks. It is the mosses and the ferns that begin to take advantage of these cracks and the tiny beginning of soil the lichens have created. The mosses are first to get microscopic filaments into these cracks and so make way for the ferns, which come later. As the rock cracks and crumbles, and the plants die and decay, bacteria are working on this dead matter, which mixes with the rock fragments to produce the first real soil, and a thin skin spreads over the rock surface. By this time, another primitive plant, the liverwort (see picture), has begun to help with the soil-building. Peel this back from the rock and it is indeed as if you were skinning it to show the layer of soil underneath.

Generations of liverworts have gradually decomposed the rock surface, added organic material, and produced about a half-inch of soil, shown under part of plant peeled back from rock surface.—*Photo courtesy U.S. Department of Agriculture.*

This wonderful forming of the life-giving soil takes much longer than you probably imagine. Before even the first lichens can grow on a rock hundreds of years have to pass while the water of rain and snow in combination with changes in daily and seasonal temperature work on the rock surface to weaken its rigidity by expansion and contraction. The greatest force is exerted when water gets into the tiniest of cracks and then freezes and expands into ice. Soon more and more almost invisible cracks appear and some tiny flakes break off. With this beginning the first lichens take hold.

The surface layers of the rock continue to be leached or washed out by rainwater, and both oxidation and hydration continue to soften the rock while some beginning action is started by weak acids, such as carbonic acid, produced by the lichens as they grow. A single lichen may go on living for many centuries. Unseen by us without a microscope, very tiny microscopic organisms, including bacteria, are also at work on the rock surface, producing gradually more soil, which is becoming increasingly filled with decayed organic material, the rich basis of good soil. Liverworts are plants that are particularly good at producing new soil and then protecting it by forming a protective covering over it. The soil itself becomes increasingly filled with dead and decaying bodies of both animals and plants.

By the time liverworts have appeared it may be hundreds of years since the first plants took hold on the rocks, and it may be many more hundreds of years before the soil is deep enough for a bush or small tree to find enough soil to grow on. This explains why man's careless destruction of good soil by fire, ruthless lumbering, or letting his domestic animals overgraze the soil and produce erosion is so dangerous. What man destroys in a year nature may take centuries to repair.

The picture of beech and hemlock trees working their roots into Berea grit in the picture shows another step in the formation of forest soils, but very large trees cannot grow here until the soil gets deeper, as they cannot form a deep enough base with their roots to hold straight their heavy weight. Deeper soil is beginning to form in the next two photographs, in the latter with enough depth to support a 95-year-old pine stand. The first picture shows the surface of deep mulch caused by a myriad dying and dead plant parts that fall down from the trees above, or by the death of smaller plants such as the low bushes, herbs, mushrooms and so forth that grow on the forest floor. All are, year by year, adding depth to the skin of the world.

Small hemlock and beech trees helping form soil on rock of Berea grit.—*Photo courtesy Cleveland Museum of Natural History.*

Mulch and dead leaves on forest floor.—*Photo courtesy U.S. Department of Agriculture.*

What Humus Does for Soil

It is good to take a trowel with you into a wood or forest and dig down to see the appearance of the soil for a foot or more below the surface. Here again the earth is talking to you, telling you of the work that has been done to create this fine material, telling of the richness of the soil and its meaning to the trees that rise above it. Darkness in the soil means there is much humus, and the mixture of this dead organic matter with fine rock particles does two things vital to good growth of plant life. One is to keep the soil open so that water can seep down easily into it and be absorbed—something a soil with too much clay (mineral matter) in it cannot do because the clay hardens when it dries, producing a hardpan that may kill a growing seed and keep small amounts of water from light rains from penetrating. The second thing the good humus soil does is to allow the air and its oxygen to come down through the openings between soil particles and reach the roots, aiding their growth even as plants need the water and the minerals which humus soil holds. A sandy soil, on the other hand, may absorb water too quickly and take it too deep where small plants cannot reach it with their

Accumulation of rich humus in a 95-year-old red pine stand in Minnesota.—*Photo courtesy U.S. Forest Service.*

roots. Some plants, however, prefer sandy soil and have roots especially adapted to it. You can see these plants growing on the edges of sand dunes and beaches, producing organic decaying matter that will make some of that sand eventually evolve into better soil for other plants.

CLIMATE'S EFFECT ON SOIL AND PLANTS

Types of soils are largely determined by the climate of a region; soil types, in turn, both determine and are themselves partly determined by the plants that live on them. Remember, however, that in any given climatic region there are soils that are typical of that region, and there are also soils that are moving by evolution toward that typical type of soil. For example, a rocky hilltop may have soil just beginning to form from lichens, mosses, and liverworts. This is a very primitive soil and similar almost everywhere in rocky areas in all parts of the temperate regions. Down the slope of a hill you may find plants struggling manfully to hold in the soil and keep it from being washed away by the rains, but the steep slope may confine the soil, as yet very thin, to supporting only bushes and small trees. Such a soil may be beginning to show some of the appearance of the typical soil of the climatic region, but lighter in color because it has not as yet accumulated very much humus. Down in the valley is the most likely place to find the rich soil developed by years of silting and building of decaying plant and animal matter into the typical soil of the region.

Results of Irregular Rainfall

We should understand that the extent and regularity of rainfall, as well as the temperature and its extremes, determines much about the nature of the soil and the plants that grow in it. Most of the western United States, except for the high mountain flats and parks, and the thick rain forest of the northwest coast, has very irregular rainfall or rainfall that comes only during one part of the year, as in most of California. Such soil is often pale brown or grayish, and shows a whitish streak of calcium deposits about two feet below the surface. This is due to the dry heat of these regions, which produces a high rate of evaporation, rarely leaving much water in the soil for long. In such mainly alkaline soils, which produce the colorful alkali deserts of the West, mostly shrubs or small trees grow and not true forests. Dark soils are produced in the West wherever there have been basaltic lava flows, which are generally black in color, but even these soils are usually dry and alkaline (litmus paper turns blue if wetted and put in alkaline soil, red in acid soil) and produce few forests.

Results of Regular Rainfall

As you move farther east, the soil gradually becomes darker and less and less alkaline until it begins to turn fairly dark and a little acid in eastern Nebraska and Kansas. This is because the climate has changed to a type that has rainfall off and on all through the year, so that the soil remains damp for a long time with much less evaporation. Thus the decaying plant materials in the soil have a chance to produce acid, which is the cause of the bright fall colors in the leaves of eastern trees. The less acid and lighter-colored brown soils of the Midwest produce the grassland prairies, spotted with prairie groves of bur oak, which are found in Iowa, Illinois, eastern Oklahoma, and elsewhere in this region. Otherwise most of the East has typical acidic forest soil, which would grow trees extensively today except where man has preferred to have plowed fields or cities.

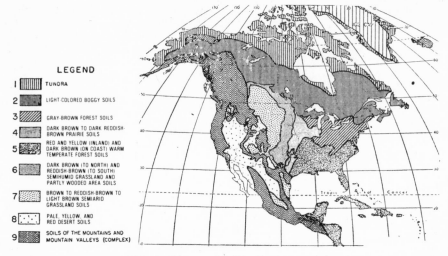

LEGEND

1 — TUNDRA

2 — LIGHT-COLORED BOGGY SOILS

3 — GRAY-BROWN FOREST SOILS

4 — DARK BROWN TO DARK REDDISH-BROWN PRAIRIE SOILS

5 — RED AND YELLOW (INLAND) AND DARK BROWN (ON COAST) WARM TEMPERATE FOREST SOILS

6 — DARK BROWN (TO NORTH) AND REDDISH-BROWN (TO SOUTH) SEMIHUMID GRASSLAND AND PARTLY WOODED AREA SOILS

7 — BROWN TO REDDISH-BROWN TO LIGHT BROWN SEMIARID GRASSLAND SOILS

8 — PALE, YELLOW, AND RED DESERT SOILS

9 — SOILS OF THE MOUNTAINS AND MOUNTAIN VALLEYS (COMPLEX)

Principal Types of Soil in North America

The northern soils of the eastern United States and Canada are dark grayish brown, or, farther north, brown below and leached whitish above, especially in boggy areas, but the greater heat of the southern states produces the typical yellow soils of the southeastern coastal plains or the reddish soils in the better-drained southern piedmonts or highlands. We can think of the sun and water rusting the iron in these southern soils to produce the brighter colors. The yellow soils have been leached of the red color by much saturation with water.

Here is a simple chart to show some of the main soils of North America and their relations to climate and to the kinds of plants that grow on them. Use it to help read the signs in the woods that tell of the relationship between soils and plants.

Soil Chart of North America

Type of soil	Geographic location	Typical plants	Signs
Pale-colored alkali soil with calcium deposits.	Dryer parts of West, desert or near-desert.	Brush, cactus (in south), small, rather gnarled trees in little woods.	Small, tough leaves to protect against drying; often spines to protect against grazing animals.
Browner-colored alkali soils, but still with calcium deposits.	Great Plains (soil light brown in west, a little darker east).	Taller grass in east, short grass in west.	Cottonwoods and willows forming woods along streams; juniper woods in Far West, edge of Great Plains.
Red and yellow soils (reds show good drainage; sandy yellow poor drainage).	Red soil in uplands of the southern states, yellow soil in the lowlands.	Oaks, tulip trees, and pines in uplands; pines in coastal plains. Bald cypresses and insect-eating plants in lowland swamps.	Poor soils allowing mainly secondary-type trees to grow on them; swamps of low-lands with insect-eating plants because of little oxygen.

Soil Chart of North America (continued)

Type of soil	Geographic location	Typical plants	Signs
Soils usually black above, brown or reddish below.	Tall grass prairies of central U.S.	Tall grass, but with bur oak woods forming islands.	Grass surrounding oak-hickory-hawthorn islands showing struggle between wet and dry climates.
Gray brown topsoil over brown lower soil.	Most of northeastern states and southeastern Canada.	Pines, hemlocks, maples, firs, spruces, birches, beech, ash.	Rainfall and snowfall usually heavy enough to create very thick woods, rich soil.
Whitish or grayish topsoil with brown subsoil.	The great north woods, north from Maine and northern Minnesota.	Spruce, firs, tamaracks, birches, pines, aspens.	Thick, dark forests with little undergrowth; tamarack bogs stifling most other plant life with acid water.

HOW ANIMALS ENRICH THE SOIL

A final factor to be noted about the nature of soils is the part played by small animals and insects in improving the aeration and quality of soils. The picture shows how these creatures burrow deep into the soil to make their nests. This not only helps bring air down to plant roots, but allows the water to sink in quickly instead of staying on or running off the surface, thus storing water below ground for use by the roots. Furthermore, these creatures carry organic materials in the form of food and nesting material below the surface, and some of them die there; thus all contribute to the enrichment of the soil. The great trees gather strength from this good in the soil and soar to the high skies. Digging with a trowel in the soil, you will uncover many signs of this underground life. Just be careful about uncovering the yellow jackets!

THE DISASTER OF SOIL EROSION

Soil is built up in two main ways. The first we have already seen in the slow accumulation of broken-up mineral matter mixed with decaying plant and animal matter. The second way is by water or wind carrying soil already built out over the earth surface and depositing it elsewhere. This movement of soil is one area's loss and another area's gain. If there is only a modest amount of this movement, it is not too bad, as the lost soil can be replaced by the plants that grow in the area and drop their dead leaves and branches on the ground or let fall their bodies onto the earth in a death that brings new life. But, when the soil movement is very fast, as it is in great floods or dust storms, and on any hillside that has been swept too bare of plant cover by fire, overgrazing, or overcutting, then the soil loss can become a double disaster. This is because the floods bring down so much silt and gravel and water that the trees below die even as do the trees above whose roots have been swept bare by the furious rain (see photo at the end of Chapter 2). Such a disaster came to the Bull Flat redwood area in northwestern California, where many great redwood trees were knocked down or drowned out by the flooding silt that came down from hillsides where lumbermen had too recklessly cleared away the trees.

Life in soil, showing yellow jacket, ant, and chipmunk nests and tunnels.—*Photo courtesy American Museum of Natural History.*

As we read the woods we need to see and understand both how soil is destroyed and how it is saved by the cooperation between it and the plant cover. If we watch bare soil when it is struck by the rain, we see each drop creating a small explosion where it hits, as both water and soil are knocked into the air by the blow (see photo on p. 36). If it is a heavy rain, the drops are fairly large and hit with considerable force. Park a newly washed car on bare ground where there is no plant cover and see what happens when a good strong rain comes. You will find that, while the upper part of the car remains shiny, the fenders and sides have been thoroughly dirtied by bits of mud often thrown up several feet by the splashing water. On a slope such constant splashing begins to churn up the soil like an automatic mixer beating up a milkshake so that the soil mixes with the water like a cream and then begins to run down the hill. If it becomes liquid enough and runs fast enough, it begins to form gullies, which get deeper and then combine to make even deeper gullies like the one shown in the

Raindrop hits unprotected soil, splashing up soil and carrying earth particles with it.—
Photo courtesy U.S. Department of Agriculture.

picture. The loss of soil under continued destruction of this sort can become so bad that only much work by men and a century or more of rebuilding by the plants will return the good earth that has been lost.

What Makes Soil Resist Erosion

The mineral content of soil helps determine how fast it may be eroded by water. The four major components of soil are water, air, organic material, and mineral material. The mineral material can be divided again into four main divisions: (1) gravel, (2) sand, (3) silt, and (4) clay, each made up of smaller and smaller particles. *ORGANIC MATERIAL AND MULCHES*   The gravel and sand on a slope are easily washed away by water, the silt less so and the clay least of all, but all four are washed away more easily than soil that has about an equal amount or more of organic material in it. This is because the organic material combines with the clay and silt often chemically to produce a spongelike quality that absorbs water instead of merely traveling with it.

Severe gully erosion near Kirkland Lake, Ontario.—*Photo courtesy Ontario Department of Lands and Forests.*

Thus, bad erosion of the soil cannot happen nearly as easily where plants have cooperated with the ground in producing rich soil with large percentages of organic matter in it. Still less can the soil be moved if it is covered with a heavy mulch of litter and leaf mold. We can think of this as a healthy earth skin, equivalent to the good skin on the hand of a healthy man. If the man's skin remains uncut or damaged, it wards off disease from outside and protects the body well, but, if a cut is made in the skin and this cut is not tended properly, then a disease can enter and spread to the whole body, eventually killing it. In the same way in the forest, if a cut or other destruction of the trees happens over a wide enough area and nothing is done about healing the endangered area, the wound in the plant cover creates a corresponding wound in the earth, a gully, caused by too much rain hitting unprotected soil on a slope, and too much runoff sweeping away plants and soil down below.

THE DIFFERENCE THAT TREES MAKE   I visited the Yolla Bolly Mountains of northwestern California twice on long camping trips into its wilderness areas in 1940 and 1941. The forest and soil cover at that time was perfect, deep with leaf mold and litter, the streams running crystal clear and jumping with rainbow trout and other stream life. I came back in 1964, not long after a terrible storm had hit the area following several years of heavy logging by lumber companies, and saw incredible destruction. Bulldozers and heavy trucks had cut gashlike roads into the mountainsides, increasing erosion (see Ruthless Logging under Man's Wasteful Practices in Chapter 5), and huge mudslides and rockslides had not only swept away large parts of the roads but many trees of the forest as well, all because the ground was not enough protected by good soil, mulch, and trees. It should be remembered that the trees themselves form an umbrella that protects the soil from being hit by a furious rain and so causes the water to fall gently into the forest litter and mulch and seep gently into the good soil.

The post oak, shown in the following photo, illustrates the great power a single tree has in preventing erosion with its roots and the litter it lets fall, but the picture also shows what happens when other nearby trees are destroyed and do not remain to cooperate with the single oak in holding soil. The earth has been torn by erosion all around this tree, but the oak has fought valiantly to protect its own. This is a common sight where trees have been widely cut down by man and only a few are left standing. Before such erosion starts, wise foresters and lumbermen rush in to cover the soil with mulch (see New Lumbering Ways That Save the Woods in Chapter 5) and plant new young trees to take up the job the older, cut-down trees were doing of holding the soil.

The root system of a kind of tree often determines where it is found, and also the kind of soil that is found under it. The hemlock and beech trees growing in Berea grit shown earlier in this chapter and the virgin redwoods shown under Pacific Coastal Coniferous Forests in Chapter 7 are very different, but they have two things in common: both are on comparatively flat land in the midst of rather thick forests. Thus they do not need a deep root system to protect them against winds or hold them upright on a steep slope. Particularly is this true of the trees growing in Berea grit, which have only very shallow soil above a hard rock layer, and would be blown down very quickly if the sheltering trees around them were taken away. On the other hand, trees such as the windswept balsam fir shown under What Wind Does in Chapter 2 and the beach and bishop pines shown under Pacific Coastal Coniferous Forests in Chapter 7 must have very deep tap (central) roots, plus strong side roots, in order to hold the trees even partly upright against the storm winds that strike them in such exposed positions. Thus, just by looking at the shape and position of a tree, whether

Post oak tree trying to hold down valuable soil, but without help from other trees.— *Photo courtesy U.S. Forest Service.*

on a slope or on a flat, in the open or on an overhanging cliff, or among crowded trees, we can tell what kind of root system it is likely to have.

The tremendous strength of plant growth is illustrated in the accompanying picture, which shows a yellow pine tree that has literally thrust itself up through almost solid rock. The terrific struggle involved in driving through the crack in the rock has twisted its trunk as it grew, like a wrestler twisting his muscles in an all-out struggle against a mighty opponent. We can make a good guess that, even as the trunk of the tree had to struggle up through the rock, so the roots had to force their way down narrow crannies in the rock to reach soil beneath where the life-giving water and minerals could be found. In such fashion have rocks weighing tons been lifted or split by a single tree!

In the battle of plants to save and build soil man can either help or destroy by a few acts of wisdom or foolishness (see Chapter 5). But left alone, even after a severe fire has destroyed most of the trees of an area, plants rebuild the soil, step by step, bringing in different plant communities for each step in the job in a process that is called succession (see Chapter 6), creating a deeper and deeper soil until the final, or climax, community rules the land. You will, in time, be able to dig in a particular soil with a trowel and tell at a glance whether you are near the beginning, the middle, or the end of the wonderful process of plants building soil to create the best possible conditions for growth.

LAND, ICE, AND SNOW MOVEMENTS

Earth, sand, snow, and ice move in many ways to affect the life of trees and woods. And the trees, on their side, combine with themselves and other plants to slow up or stop the movement of earth, sand, snow, and ice. It is a battle going on over all our land, and where the plant armies lose the fight, mankind also loses, for desertlike places spread wherever the beautiful green of the flowering earth is destroyed. We can see the signs and marks of this battle and chart the advance and retreat of the action in many woods we may visit.

Shifting Sand Dunes

Both sand and earth (or dust) are moved by winds. Strong winds, carrying great clouds of dust, have moved the vast deposits of loess into central China, and similar deposits into our central states. In the dry 1930's such clouds of dust could be seen for a thousand miles or more on the Great Plains. Much good soil was lost and trees

Twisted ponderosa pine writhing up out of solid rock in Colorado.—*Photo courtesy U.S. Forest Service.*

were killed by the dust being piled upon them. On a somewhat smaller scale we can see the same thing happening with the movement of sand dunes and the attempts of trees and other plants to tie the dunes down.

Sand dunes are found not only along ocean, gulf, and bay shores, but also on the shores of great inland lakes and even far away from water in the hearts of deserts. Being made of loose sand, generally hard white silica sand, they are easily moved by a strong wind, which picks up the sand grains and carries them forward, building new sand dunes where there were none before. Nothing in our landscape is so much like an invading army as the sand dunes marching over the land and often destroying whole forests, as can be seen in the photograph.

Certain plants help stabilize or hold back the advance of sand dunes. These plants, particularly certain grasses, are often used by men in their battle against the advance of the dunes. The grasses usually get the first start at holding down the dunes, but bushes and trees are also needed to continue the process. Often, down near ocean and lake shores, we see lines and ranks of all these plants fighting to get a firm grip on the sand and prevent it from moving.

On the other hand, the wind, coming off the wide waters, may have hundreds of miles of clear area to build up its strength, especially in a storm, so that it hits the land with great force and begins to try to find weaknesses in the battle line of the plants. This it does not do consciously, of course, but by the mere fact that a strong gale naturally begins to move loose things wherever it finds them. Once the wind finds a weak spot in the army of plants holding the sand, it begins to worry it as a terrier does a rat, moving more and more sand and covering more and more plants with it until a sand dune blowout is created (see picture). We can find signs of many an old or new blowout wherever sandy beaches and dunes are found encroaching on neighboring forests. Wherever such blowouts occur, man needs to work with pick and shovel and plant young grass, herbs, shrubs, and trees to try to stabilize the

Sand dune overwhelming mature Sitka spruce trees on Oregon coast.—*Photo courtesy U.S. Department of Agriculture.*

Sand Dune Blowout

wild dune. Taming dunes in this way is very similar to attempts to tame a wild and wayward horse, and man does not always win in either case.

Landslides and Earthquakes

That the land we walk on is not the stable thing we usually imagine it to be is quickly proved to any person who finds himself standing on land shaken by a violent earthquake or moving beneath him because of a landslide. The quiverings, shakings, and slides are often accompanied by a terrifying rumble or roar. Trees are moved or destroyed by landslides and earthquakes, and we can often tell the signs of their action and see the results long after the actual event has happened. Of course, an earthquake may actually trigger a landslide, especially if the earthquake takes place in or immediately after a period of wet weather when the soil of a hillside is so heavy with water that it is ready to slip down over the underlying rock when something happens to shake it loose. At such times trees of a hillside may be moved and destroyed. Trees are also moved or destroyed on flat lands by earthquakes violent enough to form large cracks in the earth, which may actually open beneath a tree and swallow it whole as if it were engulfed by a gigantic whale!

Another sign of a recent severe earthquake is a line of trees standing at a strange angle and yet giving no evidence of having been attacked by a strong wind, which would have bent their branches or trunks out of shape. The roll of an earthquake across the ground may have stopped at a point where the trees were tipped at an angle. The trunk of such a tree, if it continues to live, will then turn at an angle in order to grow straight up once more, an elbowlike effect that lasts for all of its life.

Landslide down hill, sweeping away part of woods.—*Photo courtesy U.S. Forest Service.*

Trees moving down a hill in a landslide (see picture) may have the same thing happen to them, or they may be buried and killed. The landslide tears out a part of the plant cover on a hill, much as does a sand dune blowout, and then nature, sometimes helped by man, moves in to bring new plants to the barren hillside. This may be very difficult, as often the landslide has cut the soil down to practically bare rock. To help the process of rebuilding, man may need to move in and dig holes in the hill where young bushes and trees can be planted with soil and fertilizer put around them to help stabilize the slide area. Special grasses and herbs are also helpful. This may have to be done quickly and thoroughly, as otherwise one or more bad gullies will soon be worn by the rain in the hillside and further deterioration of the landscape will take place. From the knowledge given here, you should be able to take a close look at a hillside hurt by a landslide and judge whether it is showing signs of a healthy recovery or whether it is in grave danger of gullying. A former slide eventually may be so covered by plants as to be almost completely disguised, but you can usually tell where it has been by finding twisted live or dead trees, the latter usually half-buried in the ground, or by noticing the dip in the land caused by the slide and observing the area covered by tree cover of the fast-growing species that usually spring up first in partially destroyed areas (see Secondary Plant Succession in Chapter 6).

Glaciers

Glaciers have covered enormous areas of our country in past millennia, but modern glaciers are comparatively few, found in the highest mountains or far north in Alaska, Greenland, and northern Canada. However, the ancient glaciers have left their effect on the land and on the forests even though they disappeared from most of their former extent about eight thousand or more years ago. This is because they did, and the modern glaciers still do, create soil that eventually becomes ideal for trees to grow on, and because they left hollows in the earth's surface, made by their tremendous grinding weight when they moved, that are now filled with lakes. In some places one can actually see forests that follow the lines where an ancient glacier had been and had left its moraines or deposits of ground-up and potentially good soil. Though largely made of crumbling rock and gravel in the beginning,

Palisade Glaciers in Sierras, on shade-protected north-facing slopes, with whitebark pines below and Summit Lake in foreground.—*Photo courtesy U.S. Forest Service.*

the action of plants eventually breaks this matter down into good humus-filled soil. The accompanying picture shows how trees are beginning to grow on the moraines of gravel and rock pushed down by the Palisade Glaciers in the Sierras. Of course, smaller plants, such as the lichens, mosses, and liverworts and then herbs and ferns had to begin the soil-building.

How the great and little lakes influence the climate, moderating surrounding dry areas with moisture, has already been discussed under Glacial Lakes in Chapter

Avalanche tracks of snowslide in upper subalpine zone, Colorado Rockies, with subalpine firs and Engelmann spruces.—*Photo by Richard G. Beidlemen.*

1. So trees have been able to spread deeper into the heart of the continent because of the influence of these glacier-made lakes.

Snowslides

As snow piles on snow on the steeper slopes of the mountains, it grows greatly in weight, especially if it is a wet snow. When the air is very cold in winter, the water in the snow is all frozen, and it sticks tight to the slope even as water thrown on a window when the temperature is below freezing freezes tightly to the vertical glass. But if a warm day comes, as spring approaches, the heat of the sun may begin to melt the surface snow and send little rills of water running down below until they break loose the ice that is clinging to the rocks and gravel underneath. At this point something terrible may begin to move—a great snowslide. The slipping snow gathers momentum and suddenly hurtles down the slope with a vast roar, not only knocking down trees and trapping and smothering any animals or men caught in its path, but also digging up some of the earth itself.

One of the signs we see of such work the next summer is shown in the picture of a trail dug by an avalanche in the earth. Often also we see the forms of dead trees knocked about and left sprawling on the slope. The gash in the earth must be healed by plant growth or it may begin to gully and get worse.

CHAPTER FOUR

Effects of Fire
and Rebirth

FIRE, THE GREAT ally and great enemy of man, is usually nothing but the enemy of plants. However, small plants may benefit by the destruction of large plants by fire, since too much shade for the small plants is removed, and sometimes trees, such as the lodgepole pine in the West and the jack pine in the Middlewest, are helped to give off seeds by fire and so start new generations. Thus a forest that is destroyed by flames is supplanted, at least temporarily, by grasses and herbs that spring up in the new well-lighted areas. Also, both trees and wildlife may benefit from slow-moving ground fires that are allowed to burn at times of the year when the forest is damp enough so that only the debris on the forest floor and some of the undergrowth is destroyed while the trees themselves are unharmed.

In the old days the Indians often started fires for this purpose, producing park-like forests where grass grew that attracted deer and other plant-eating animals, and where the hunter found hunting easier because of less brush and debris. Such fires actually prevented much more dangerous crown fires from starting later by preventing brush and piles of dead limbs from going so high as to form a fire hazard up which flames could climb to the treetops.

Here and there modern foresters are beginning to utilize this secret of the Indians; so if you find such a controlled fire being managed by foresters or park rangers, or find the signs of such a fire in the ashes of charred forest debris, but without signs of serious damage to the trees, you will know the reasons. Such fires have to be used very carefully, however, as too much destruction of forest debris hurts the building of soil, and there is also danger of such fires destroying valuable young trees.

FOREST FIRE DAMAGE

Fires leave many signs in the woods, including those mentioned above, ranging from complete destruction to amazing examples of almost complete regeneration of a tree after what must have been a terrible fire. Redwood trees in particular, because of the fire-resistant nature of both their bark and wood, may show trees half-carved and eaten away by fire into their very vitals, and yet living to continue growth, even eventually growing over the wound (see photo of redwood log). Some large trees have been hollowed out enough by such a process to produce caves in which primitive man and sometimes modern hermits have lived.

Effects of Ground and Crown Fires

The fire leaping treeward in the picture is still a ground fire, moving along over the surface of the earth under the trees and feeding mainly on debris and underbrush, but it is beginning to creep up the trunks, and, if not stopped in time, may graduate into a crown fire of the type so terrible that sometimes its flames leap miles across a forest, carried by the wind, and destroying everything in their path. Even a strictly

Part of big redwood log, showing ancient fire burn in heart of tree.—*Photo by Moulin Studios, San Francisco, Calif.*

Fire in Angeles National Forest, California in 1942.—*Photo courtesy U.S. Forest Service.*

ground fire will kill many trees and bushes, but usually leaves enough living to help create an early regeneration of plants after the fire.

We can thus generally tell whether a ground, crown or intermediate-grade fire has passed by, by the extent of damage to the trees. Total death means a real crown fire, while some live trees remaining among the dead give evidence of a milder fire; a true ground fire would destroy only an occasional tree where the forest debris was thickest.

The fiery hell of a truly big fire, or even the threat of it in a lesser fire, puts such a pall of smoke and destruction over the land, when the tremendous roar and crackling of the flames seems so unstoppable, that the human spirit is depressed in an agony of sorrow. Every careless camper and hunter who has ever set or come near to setting a forest fire by a carelessly thrown match or cigarette or by making a campfire near forest debris and leaving it untended would learn a great lesson from going through the experience of fighting one of these fires. I remember as a boy, in the summer of 1933, watching from its fringes the 245,000-acre Tillamook Fire in Oregon. Called the Tilla-mook Inferno because of the incredible intensity of its flames, this was one of the great fires of history. With awe I watched a fiery cloud of burning material carried through the air on the wings of the fierce wind and land in a place a dozen miles or more from the main fire. Even where I was, at least ten miles from the nearest flames, the strong heat could be felt on my face, and the smell of smoke was terrifying!

Gloomy results of fierce forest fire in Glacier National Park, Montana.—*Photo courtesy Library of Congress.*

BEING PREPARED FOR FOREST FIRES

Danger Signs

One of the signs to watch for in the woods is the sign of imminent fire danger. You can tell it by the following things: (1) the air is dry and hot, often with a strong odor of pine pitch; (2) the grass and dead leaves underfoot crackle as you walk on them; (3) the bark peels off some trees in dry sheets so brittle they may come apart in your hands; (4) the sky seems a hot brassy blue in color; (5) the voices of animals and birds are muted or silent and, if you have sensitivity, a note of fear is evident in the little sounds they make; (6) the soil is dry and often hard, with no sign of moisture. If you see all or most of these evidences of danger, it is a good plan to get out of these woods and warn others to stay away from them until a rain comes. If there is smoke in the air and animals are running and birds flying all in one direction, then you yourself are in great danger and had better get to a place of safety, such as a river, a lake, a town, or, at least, a wide-open space of considerable extent, just as fast as possible! A crown fire, carried by a strong wind, can easily run down a fleeing man. Even a man in a car on a highway through such woods that are aflame has a good chance of being caught unless he goes in the right direction very fast.

Safety Signs

On the other hand, hearing no sound from the leaf mold as it bends like a sponge under your feet, hearing the sounds of birds singing and chattering and squirrels chittering, feeling a dampness in the bark you touch, a good smell of moisture in the air, leaves of plants green and fresh-looking—these are all signs of a forest in which fire danger is low and where you can enjoy yourself with little fear. However, the truly careless camper or hunter can set even such a forest on fire with an act of forgetfulness, so, at all times, keep your eyes, ears, and nose open for the sight or smell of smoke, and quickly notify the nearest forest service station of these signs of danger in the woods.

HOW TREES AND FORESTS SURVIVE

Legends from long ago tell how the phoenix and the thunderbird were burned to death, and then later rose gloriously alive from their ashes. Great fires constantly sweep different parts of our American wilderness, destroying beautiful forests, but nature has ways of bringing these forests back to life and man has learned how to help. This regeneration, whether helped or not by man, leaves its signs in the woods for us to see when we visit them. It is a miracle of life and the spirit that we should watch for.

Fortunately, some trees live even after a fire has swept over their forest. This may be and usually is due to some fortuitous circumstance. If the fire is a slow-moving ground fire, it may move around the tree because the litter and brush is either not near that tree or has been cleared away from it so that no large flames get near it. In this case you may notice that the tree has been scorched more or less on all sides. Another possibility is that the fire came right up almost to the tree, but was then turned back by the wind shifting direction, by rain coming, or by fire-fighters stopping the fire at this point. In any of these cases, we find signs of the tree being scorched on one side only. In still another case, the fire might have burned up the tree's trunk, but have been stopped by rain before it could kill the tree. Such a case is illustrated by the photo-

Forest fire damage two years after the fire. The tree is healing over and will probably grow to maturity, but its wood value is less and insects may attack via the wound.— *Photo courtesy American Forest Products Industries, Inc.*

graph, in which a tree is gradually growing around the old black wound made by a fire two years before.

Complications in Tree Recovery

Just like a human being recuperating from a severe wound on the body or a limb, the tree also is weak after an attack by fire. The weakness is greatest around the wound, and the tree may be attacked by fungus or other injurious plants, or by insects (see Harmful Insects and Harmful Fungi in Chapter 5). Not only insects injurious to trees, but insects injurious to man may use such places. We have an old oak on our property that had a fire attack one side long ago so that fungus was able to get into the wound and turn some of the wood rotten. A telephone man came to put in a new telephone line that went right by the tree, and, when he started to climb it, was suddenly attacked by yellow jackets, who had a nest made of holes bored in the rotting wood. I was up late that night, spraying insect poison into the holes and finally sealing up the entranceways with mud to make the place safe for him!

Nourishers of New Tree Growth

DEAD TREES AND STUMPS   Dead, burnt-out trees and stumps left by fire have their uses in starting new growth. Any fire-burnt tree begins to rot in time and is eventually knocked over by the wind. When it falls, it often breaks to pieces and these pieces continue rotting and falling apart on the ground, being riddled by insects and fungus in the process. This produces a fine mulch on the ground in which new trees can find life and growth. Thus, even though insects and fungus may be harmful to living trees that they infect, they are distinctly helpful to new plant growth after the death by fire of old trees. They are an important part of the beautiful cycle of life, death, and rebirth in the woods, endlessly revolving.

Fir seedling growing up in shelter of old stump is also protected from grazing.—*Photo courtesy U.S. Department of Agriculture.*

Dense cover of fireweed, growing up among dead timber of old Tillamook Burn, six years after fire, renews soil.—*Photo courtesy U.S. Department of Agriculture.*

Another use of a dead stump or tree is to shelter a young tree from too much sun or wind (as shown in the photo). Many a new-risen tree in the open space caused by a big forest fire has little chance to rise from the earth because its tender leaves are withered by the blazing summer sun or a wind knocks it over. The old stump, like an aging grandmother, shelters what may possibly be its own grandchild, from the enemies of heat and wind.

QUICK-GROWING WEEDS   A really terrible fire, like the famous Tillamook Inferno in Oregon described earlier in this chapter, burns with such fierceness that the soil may have most of its organic matter destroyed by the heat right down to the mineral base. After such a fire young trees have little chance to get started because they cannot find the nutrients needed. But there are plants especially adapted to grow in this kind of barren soil, such as the fireweed shown in the picture of the Tillamook Burn. These plants are a sign to us of what has happened to the soil from the fire, but they are also a sign of regeneration of that soil, for, in a few years, these quick-growing herbs die, their bodies going back into the earth to give it organic material and make humus. Soon the soil is ready for young trees to rise from it and renew the forest. In a sense, the fireweed actually gives its life for the forest to come, since, eventually, the trees will overshadow the smaller, narrow-leaved plants and cause them to die because of too much shade (see What Shade Does to Plants in Chapter 1). In the shade under the trees, in time, different small plants begin to grow whose large leaves are adapted to producing food where only a few stray rays of sunlight can find their way down to them.

Poor Conditions for Forest Renewal

Sometimes the death of a forest from fire happens on such rocky soil, or soil so leached and stripped by erosion following the fire, that the regeneration of the forest is very slow and painful. Such an area of very poor and slow regeneration of a forest is shown in the photo of the McIntyre Burn. This fire occurred sixty-five years before the picture was taken! Here are all the signs of poor and difficult soil, including old logs not even covered by new growth. The plant cover is indeed so small that rocky soil is exposed, while such trees as are growing are very widely spaced. Here is where man must lend a hand to rebuild the soil and get tree growth going again. For example, some of the more progressive lumber companies, who realize their only long-term future lies in active regeneration of burnt-over or cut-over forests, would take all the rotting logs shown in the picture and run them through a machine that would cut them and other debris into tiny pieces. These pieces would then be blown out over the land by a powerful blowing machine to form an even layer of mulch several inches deep that would begin immediately to protect the soil from erosion, and, a little later, would sink into the soil and make it into tree-growing humus.

Slope may also have something to do with the difficulty or ease of a forest starting up after a bad burn. Thus the McIntyre Burn illustrated in the picture shows a medium-steep hillside where the flow of water after a rain or a melting of snow naturally moves any loose soil down the slope. With the tree cover gone because of the fire, the erosion caused by water movement on a slope is increased, and the ability of the small grasses and herbs that grow up after a fire to prevent this erosion may not be enough. Thus a vicious circle of removal of the soil faster than it can be produced is set up, with trees prevented from coming back perhaps for centuries! Wherever gullies are starting in this soil, the long-range destruction by the fire is evident. Man may have to step in to save such a situation, a situation that too often was caused in the beginning by man himself.

Example of poor regeneration of forest 65 years after McIntyre Burn in Colorado Rockies; a few young spruce trees are coming up.—*Photo courtesy U.S. Department of Agriculture.*

Good Conditions for Forest Renewal

Contrast the picture of the McIntyre Burn with the accompanying photo. In this photograph young healthy spruce and balsam fir seedlings have sprung up in profusion where a fire raged only about ten years before. This is a natural regeneration, since the few trees that were saved from the fire were able to spread their seeds over the ground here and the soil was not too badly hurt by the fire. Being on flat land, rather than a hillside, the soil was also naturally deeper, and few rocks interfered with growth. The old burnt stumps and snags must still fall and rot away to produce still better soil, but the appearance of the young trees shows that they are bursting with energy and growth and will soon be recreating a forest to duplicate the one that was destroyed. By soon, of course, is meant in a hundred years or so, a short time in the life of these great trees!

Man could help this process by thinning out the trees when they begin to crowd each other, possibly replanting some in areas that are more barren, thus opening up the

White spruce and balsam fir seedlings are springing up with good forest regeneration where forest has been badly burned.—*Photo courtesy American Forest Products Industries, Inc.*

young forest for faster growth and at the same time spreading it. Note that the picture shows early signs of overcrowding, for some trees have branches already closely interlaced. If we remember that each individual tree spaces its branches to procure the maximum amount of sunlight and air for each leaf, we can see that this picture shows how some leaves inevitably suffer and die from lack of light in such conditions of overcrowding. Remember also that the young trees are growing in an open space where much sun can reach them because of the death of the giants. As they grow higher, the competition between them and the increase of shade will cause the lower branches to die and fall off, leaving the lower parts of the trunks bare as the mature trees begin to reach their tops into a new forest canopy. This is another sign we should watch for as the woods grow. We should, however, be aware that there are usually exceptions to every rule. Lodgepole pines, of the western mountains, for example, may have their lower limbs die under increasing shade conditions, but the dead branches continue to hang onto the trees for a long time, making a lodgepole pine forest rather unpleasant to walk through!

Nurse Trees

Often when one kind of forest is wiped out by fire, a different kind of woods grows up in its place. This is a part of plant succession (see Chapter 6), but the result, at least temporarily, may be that good timber trees are replaced by trees that have little lumber value. The accompanying photograph shows where a forest of longleaf, loblolly, and slash pines, all useful timber trees, in North Carolina, was destroyed by fire and is being replaced by scrub hardwoods. These scrub trees, such as sweet bay, sassafras, blackjack oak, bear oak, Carolina buckthorn, sumac, and rusty black haw, have little timber value. However, they are faster-growing trees than the pines, and spring up more quickly on poorer soil, partly ruined by fire. In time the original pines will probably rise above them and drown them out with shade, but the process is a long and slow one. Fortunately, the scrub trees do a job of rebuilding the soil to make it food for the pines.

The nonproductive nature of these scrub woods tells us what a monument to carelessness was the fire that destroyed the original pine forest and left its blackened skeletons to be surrounded by these lower trees. Such a scrub forest, with its stiff or even spiny-limbed trees, is as difficult to penetrate as a jungle, but is a good hiding place for wild animals.

Scrub hardwoods of blackjack oak, chokecherry, black haw, etc. growing up to replace valuable pine forest lost in fire.—*Photo courtesy American Forest Products Industries, Inc.*

Scrub woods like these can sometimes be thought of as foster mothers or nurse trees for both the land and for the young new coniferous trees that begin to grow up in their shelter as the soil gets better. Not needing the fine soil of the large coniferous trees, they act as forerunners, soil builders, and shade furnishers for the greater trees to come. Usually swifter-growing, they are also short-lived, so that their dying limbs and bodies soon begin to form mulch and organic matter to enrich the soil that was partly destroyed by fire.

ASPENS   Probably the greatest foster-mother nurse tree in America, and certainly one of the finest rebuilders of soil, is the aspen, both quaking aspen (associated with most of our northern and western coniferous forests), and the large-toothed aspen (found mainly in the Northeast). Aspen comes in quickly after a fire and grows faster than almost any other tree. Soon its bright green leaves are "shivering" in the slightest breeze, and a new area of soil is protected from erosion and being made ready for the return of the larger trees that were destroyed by fire. See the photograph showing aspen trees sheltering a new generation of young spruce trees, which will eventually kill their foster mothers with shade and raise a new canopy of dark green spires to the western sky.

Every fall the aspens' twirling leaves flutter down like yellow or golden rain to add mulch to the soil that will help the young conifers grow, and every summer the nurse trees allow just enough sunlight through their tops to help the growth of the young spruce or fir trees that have started to grow below.

The amazing thing about the aspen trees is that their weaknesses are also their strengths. They are very short-lived trees, with wood that is soft and brittle and which easily rots. But this is good for creating new soil, and the fast growth of these trees in shallow or fire-hurt soil makes them extremely successful in taking over after a fire and rebuilding the soil. No matter how bad the fire has been, or how deep it has killed the humus in the soil, making it little more than sterile mineral grains, the aspen seems somehow to take hold and grow. Its very presence is a sign to us of poor soil and of recent fiery destruction, because it can compete successfully with the conifers only where the soil is poor or the greater trees and their shadow-making heights and leaves

Young spruce trees growing up under protection of quaking aspen nurse trees in the New Mexico Rockies.—*Photo courtesy U.S. Forest Service.*

have been cut down by man or fire. It also can grow in damper soil near streams where the conifers do not like the moisture. The short-lived, quickly rotting aspens take over the almost pure mineral soil and build it up quickly into soil capable of raising conifers in a very few years, by adding mulch and eventually humus to the ground below. Meanwhile, they do a yeoman job of stopping erosion with their roots and their canopy of leaves that filter down the rain until it drops softly onto the soil. Around their feet grasses and herbs flourish because their shade does not keep out the sun like the thick needles of most conifers.

Notice the signs these trees give us in the woods. The comparatively light shade of the aspens and similar quick-growing deciduous trees protects but does not overshadow the young coniferous trees. On the other hand, the thick needles of the pines, firs, and other conifers are often like a dark curtain between the sky and the earth, drowning out other trees with their shade and so often producing the dominant, or climax, forest. The aspens thus may sacrifice their lives for the conifers, though some always act as hangers-on about the fringes of the mighty forests. This strange helping of the big trees by the lesser in an almost perfect cooperation makes one feel that this is all part of an extraordinary plan. Whatever is the cause, man can be thankful that it exists, for our forests would be in much greater danger from fire if it were not for this remarkable partnership.

BIRCHES   Other similar foster-mother or nurse trees can be found in different parts of America, but perhaps the most important besides the aspens are the birches, the jack pines, the scrub oaks, and the hawthorns. The birches are the queens of the north woods, especially the canoe birches, the gleaming white trunks like slender maidens dressed in ermine with dark trimmings. They too are quick growers, like the aspens, and spring up in open places left by fires or lumbering, rising out of infertile soils to make them fertile by their death and decay.

JACK PINES   It is strange to find a conifer acting the part of a nurse tree after a fire has destroyed other conifers, but all around the Great Lakes region the jack pines move in to replace their larger relatives, like elfin cousins, taking over the burnt soils where red and white pines were once the rulers (see picture). Though its wood is weak,

Natural jack pine regeneration of area burned ten years earlier.—*Photo courtesy Ontario Department of Lands and Forests.*

soft, and light like that of most other nurse trees, the jack pine's often twisted form presents a tough resistance to the wind, and it has an amazing ability to spring up on sandy, almost completely mineral soils that the bigger conifers shun. It is not as swift a grower as the aspen, though it grows fairly rapidly during its first few years. Later it slows up considerably with the result that the young trees of the red and white pines it has sheltered may soon begin to surpass it in height and eventually drown it out with shade and replace it. However, the jack pine, like the aspen, is far more ready for fire than its big cousins, for its characteristic but strange-looking curved or humpbacked cones are not likely to open until the heat of the forest fire forces them to. Then out spring the seeds to the ground, those that avoid the heat ready to spring forth with new life in the fire-scorched ground when the greater trees are dead and charred.

CHAPTER FIVE

How Animals and Man Fashion the Woodlands

THE WOODS AND forests of America are a part of the great web of all life, and in this web almost all living things influence each other in one way or another. As we walk through the woods or drive slowly along a road among the trees we can watch for and understand many of the signs that tell us of this interaction.

MAMMALS AS BUILDERS AND DESTROYERS

The creatures most of us call animals, such as cats, dogs, rabbits and so forth, should really be called mammals, or four-legged animals with hair or fur and with mammary glands in the females, for they are only one part or division of the immense animal kingdom. The chart below explains some of the common signs we may see of the work of mammals in the forests and explains what causes them. There are naturally many more than there is room to show here, but, if you learn to watch carefully and have some idea of what to look for from the information given here, you will see and understand many other signs that tell of the interweaving of mammal life with plant life.

Common Animal Signs in the Woods

Visible signs	How signs are caused	Results of animal activities
Herbs and grass nibbled almost to ground.	Cattle, sheep, and jackrabbits overgraze when population is too great for range.	Removal of ground cover permits easy erosion of unprotected topsoil by storm water.
Trees and shrubs with leaves and bark eaten away to high level.	Goats, deer, and elk standing on hind legs overbrowse when population is too great for range.	Injuries to tree bark open wounds that cause insect or disease infections; killing of trees by ring-barking may start erosion.
Clawed tree bark.	Male animals make claw marks as prestige symbols. Bears, wildcats, lynxes, and mountain lions claw trees as high as possible. Bears claw to get sap.	Trees may be killed by insects or diseases entering through injuries, or stripping off bark around them; dead trees make way for erosion.
Chewed-through trunks of felled trees and bushes.	Beavers cut down shrubs and small trees for food or for making dams.	Erosion may result. However, beavers cut mainly very fast-growing trees; beaver dams in streams prevent too fast runoff, create bogs, meadows, then forests.
Dug-up soil under trees.	Bears dig soil and overturn rocks and logs to get grubs; rodents, moles dig small holes; badgers, foxes dig larger holes.	Work of bears may start erosion, especially on steep slopes; work of rodents usually helps aerate soil and brings water deeper into ground. Badgers and foxes may cause erosion.
Seeds stored in ground, under logs, etc.	Squirrels and chipmunks store nuts and seeds, but forget them often.	Though most of these seeds and nuts are eaten, enough are forgotten so that these animals help plant new trees.
Bark of tree eaten rather high up.	Porcupines feed largely on bark, especially of pines.	Trees are often ring-barked and so killed by porcupines. Dead trees may lead to erosion, but thinning sometimes helps.
Piles of animal dung.	Coyotes, foxes, wildcats, etc. often leave dung piles in favorite spots.	Fertilizes soil and makes better humus. Trees or bushes spring up in such places.

The Results of Overgrazing

The picture of adjacent woodlots shows how cattle have affected the woods by overgrazing on one side of the fence, stripping away almost all ground covering and protective plants, while the other side of the fence shows a lush undergrowth that holds in the soil and protects it against erosion. Erosion has not yet started in this picture, but it soon would appear on the steeper slopes if the cattle were allowed to continue overgrazing here. The gully shown in the picture of Sequoia National Forest was started by such overgrazing. As the gully gets bigger, trees are undermined and begin to fall into it, destroying more and more of the forest and stripping off the good topsoil so that new trees cannot grow here.

Cattle have overgrazed one woodlot in this picture, but woodlot on other side of fence shows natural growth.—*Photo courtesy American Forest Products Industries, Inc.*

The Results of Beaver Work

See the picture showing where a beaver has cut down an aspen tree by chewing through the trunk, cutting out large chips of wood with its powerful and sharp incisor teeth. Such trees are cut into shorter lengths by the beaver and then dragged down to the beaver pond to be used for strengthening the dam. Smaller trees and bushes are cut for food value in the bark and dragged into the water, where they are weighted down with rocks and mud to hold them below the coming ice and store them for winter food. Where beavers become too populous in an area, they may do widespread damage to streamside trees and so increase erosion. But, in

Erosion started by overgrazing followed by lumbermen skidding out trees in Sequoia National Forest, California.—*Photo courtesy U.S. Forest Service.*

Work of beaver cutting aspen tree.—*Photo courtesy Canadian Wildlife Service.*

some areas, foresters have actually imported beavers into the mountains in order to encourage them to build dams that store water and prevent too much rapid runoff of winter snow water and spring rains. The pond behind the dam usually eventually fills up with silt, creating a boggy area that at last turns into a meadow and finally into a forest (see Chapter 6 on plant succession). Such a beaver pond and the house made of sticks that stands in the middle of it are shown in the picture.

How Bears Hurt Trees

A large male bear can do considerable damage to a tree by clawing it as high as he can, then rubbing his back against it and leaving hairs as a warning sign to other males that he is the boss of this wood. Usually such clawing is on one side of the tree only and does not actually kill the tree, though it allows the tree to be attacked easily by insects and diseases that may eventually kill it. Other bears, however, may really kill trees by completely girdling them in order to get at the sweet sap. This is

Beaver house and pond. Beaver pond eventually fills up with silt, producing soil for tree growth. Dam helps stop erosion.—*Photo courtesy U.S. Department of Agriculture.*

Twenty-four-inch Douglas fir girdled by bears stripping off bark to get at the sap for food in the springtime; tree was destroyed.—*Photo courtesy American Forest Products Industries, Inc.*

particularly true in the springtime when bears have just come out of hibernation and find very little food to eat in the way of grubs, tubers, or insects. Therefore, a tree with sweet sap, like a maple, gives a tempting temporary food supply. But such work quickly kills the tree and several trees killed starts erosion.

How Wildcats Hurt Trees

Members of the cat family, such as wildcats, lynxes, and mountain lions, also claw the trees, but never for food, entirely for reasons of prestige. A big male shows off his height and strength by such clawing, warning other males away from his territory. Damage is usually done to the tree, opening up wounds for insect and fungus attack, but not as bad as the work of bears. The claw marks of the big cats are much thinner than the claw marks of the bear.

How Deer Hurt Trees

Deer and goats are browsers rather than grazers, like sheep and cattle, though they do some grazing. In winter, especially, when the soil and grasses are covered with snow in the woods, the deer must browse on the bark and leaves of trees in order to live (see picture). If the deer herds are small, such browsing does not do too much harm to the forest, but large herds may be so numerous that many trees are girdled of bark and killed. Signs of dead and dying trees in forests can quickly be determined to be the work of deer when you notice the high stripping away of the leaves and the teeth marks that are high on the tree but never as high as the teeth marks of porcupines are found.

If deer signs are numerous on the trees, they may be telling us that the natural enemies of the deer, the mountain lions, have been so killed off by bounty hunters that too few of them are around to keep the deer population down to a level that is balanced with the food in the forest. Such overpopulation caused great damage to the fir and pine forests of the Kaibab Plateau north of the Grand Canyon when the mountain lions there were almost entirely killed off, along with wolves and coyotes. The deer jumped from a comfortable 3,500 to a staggering 100,000 in approximately eighteen years from 1907 to 1925. Thus does man, in his ignorance, upset the balance of nature and cause destruction.

Watch for these and many other signs animals leave in the woods, and soon you will be able to tell exactly what the signs mean and be able to predict what might happen in the next few years. Overgrazing, overbrowsing, too much beaver work, all have their built-in warning systems that the true woods reader can understand and perhaps pass on to other men who can stop or control the damage.

NATURE'S GOOD SAMARITANS, THE BIRDS

Birds leave their signs throughout our woods of what they have done and also show by their actions whether they are doing good or harm to the woods. Most birds are bringers of well-being to our forests and so are the allies of man. These certainly should not be shot, but should be protected. Only a few are actually harmful. The chart below will show you some common bird signs you may expect to see in the woods and what they mean to the trees.

White-tailed deer standing up to reach jack pine needles, the only food it can find in the deep snow. Its favorite food is cedar boughs.—*Photo courtesy Michigan Department of Conservation.*

Common Bird Signs in the Woods

Visible signs	Birds causing signs	Results of bird activities
Holes in live trees. (See picture showing how a woodpecker has stored acorns for future use.)	Birds possessing strong, sharp bills for drilling in wood, such as woodpeckers (including flickers) and sapsuckers.	Woodpeckers that bore into trees to find insect grubs usually help trees; some also store nuts in these holes. Sapsuckers bore into trees to suck sap and may hurt trees.
Seeds dropped far from home tree.	Woodpeckers (including flickers), jays, waxwings, sparrows, goldfinches, grosbeaks, siskins, crossbills, etc.	Such seed-eating birds often spread tree generations by dropping seeds; some pass through intestines and are still viable, starting new trees.
Holes in dead trees.	Woodpeckers (including flickers).	These holes help to speed decay of dead trees; large holes are used for nests.
Evidence of insect-eating. (There are few signs after act, except holes in trees.)	Warblers, vireos, jays, woodpeckers, creepers, nuthatches, thrushes, kinglets, etc.	Since most insects found around trees are generally plant eaters and so harmful, birds that eat insects help trees and need protection. However, some insects eaten are good insects.
Fertilizing of flowers.	Mainly hummingbirds. (A few other birds may do it accidentally.)	Hummingbirds dip their long bills into flowers to get nectar and help fertilize flowers, mainly of subtropical trees, tupelos, catalpas, etc.
Bird droppings.	All birds in forest.	Birds often have favorite places to make their droppings. Such places develop good organic soil and are good places for trees to grow.

Woodpeckers stored these acorns in holes as reserve food supply in Jeffrey pine trunk. Holes were probably made originally to hunt for underbark grubs —*Photo courtesy U.S. Forest Service.*

HARMFUL INSECTS

Insects have among them some of the greatest allies and also the greatest enemies of man on this earth. In our forests, insects leave their signs everywhere. We can often look at these signs and know immediately whether they are good or bad, and sometimes prophesy whether greater evil or good is coming. Because the kinds of insects are so very numerous, the chart below shows only a few of the signs they leave in the woods, but it will help you interpret many of those not actually listed here that you will see. Many diseases are carried by insects and one of these is discussed here rather than separately.

Common Insect Signs in the Woods

Visible signs	Insects causing signs	Results of insect activities
Tiny holes in bark	Bark beetles (Scolytidae), mainly larvae, and other beetles, such as long-horned.	Holes through bark lead to other holes in cambium of wood where tree may be girdled and killed; also carry diseases, such as Dutch elm disease.
Insect eggs and pupae (cocoons, etc.), found in cracks in bark, on twigs, leaves, etc. (Eggs are usually white, while pupae may be larger and darker.)	Clearwing moths, tortricid moths, tent caterpillars, scale insects, aphids, lace bugs, etc.	Both eggs and pupae are in a quiet stage and so harmless, but from them often come larvae and adult insects that attack trees.
Galleries seen between bark and wood or in holes in wood.	Bark beetles, turpentine beetles, anobiid beetles, clearwing moth larvae, carpenter moth larvae, darkling beetle larvae, engraver beetles, long-horned beetle larvae, larvae of the metallic wood borer beetles, etc.	All these insects hurt trees by destroying the cambium (where the sap rises), often killing them. (Some other insects, such as checkered beetle larvae and ichneumon fly larvae, attack and kill, or parasitize, these harmful insects.)

Larvae and web nest of the eastern tent caterpillar *(Malacosoma americanum)* on wild cherry.—*Photo courtesy U.S. Department of Agriculture.*

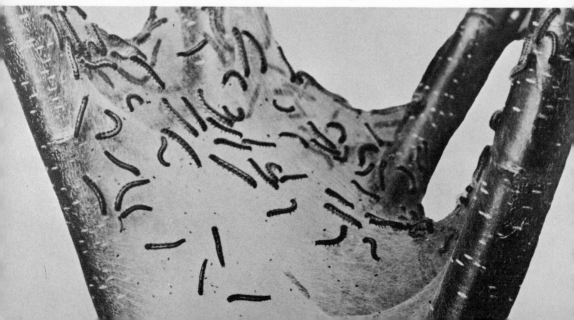

Common Insect Signs in the Woods (continued)

Visible signs	Insects causing signs	Results of insect activities
Webs on leaves.	Tent caterpillars, webworms (see photo of tent caterpillar web nest).	Put webs over leaves and branches for protection from enemies; feed on leaves, often stripping tree.
Large holes in leaves.	Many moth and butterfly caterpillars, tree crickets, walkingsticks, buprestid beetles, etc.	Trees stripped of leaves by these insects often die.
Tiny holes or tunnels under leaf layers (appearing as light network).	Leaf-mining moth larvae, crane fly larvae, leaf beetle larvae, fruit fly larvae, larvae of the metallic wood borer beetles, weevil larvae, etc.	Leaves are gradually destroyed by this process and trees injured, but not usually as seriously as by above insects.
Leaves with discolored parts.	Insects with sucking mouths, such as aphids, white flies, scale insects, leaf and plant bugs, etc.	Leaves are sucked of fluids by these insects and eventually die, possibly killing tree.
Holes and discoloring in fruits.	Casebearer moth larvae, eucosmid moth larvae, fruit flies, small fruit flies, scale insects, soldier fly larvae, etc.	All harm the fruit, cutting down on reproduction of trees. These insects eaten by ladybird beetles, robber flies, snake flies, vespid wasps, etc.
Holes and discoloring in roots, accompanied by droopy and sick-looking appearance of tree.	Larvae of carpenter moth, cicada, clearwing moth, click beetle, crane fly, phalaenid moth, scarab beetle, etc. Nematode worms.	Roots, if heavily infected by these insects, die and become useless to tree, eventually killing it. Although not insects, invisible nematode worms can be extremely harmful.
Small to large balls or bulges (galls) on leaves, twigs, branches that are not fruits, but are produced by adult insects laying eggs under surface or otherwise disturbing plant cells.	Larvae of clearwing moth, fruit fly, gall midge, cynipid gall wasps, leaf beetle, metallic wood borer beetle, sawfly. Also psyllids, etc.	Though galls are usually produced by injurious insects, they are not always injurious to the tree; in fact, some galls are important producers of tannic acid or various dyes, so their effect may sometimes be more good than bad.

Bark Beetles

Insects, unfortunately, often combine with tree diseases to spread them, and one of the most terrible enemies of the elms of America is the elm bark beetle (*Scolytus multistriatus*), which brings with it almost everywhere it goes, the infamous Dutch elm disease, a fungus growth that gets into the cambium and kills it. Besides the characteristic centipedelike engravings of holes made by the beetle larvae under the bark of the elms, and the "shotgun holes" in the bark where the larvae have come out to turn into full-grown beetles, the larvae also leave a distinctive rusty-colored material or mess in the tree crotches. If you ever notice these signs in an elm tree, you should give notice

White elm dying of Dutch elm disease, carried to it by bark beetles.—*Photo courtesy Ontario Department of Lands and Forests.*

Galleries of the grubs of the bark beetle that carries Dutch elm disease, showing intricate design.—*Photo courtesy U.S. Department of Agriculture.*

to the nearest agricultural office so it can arrange to prevent the beetles from spreading farther. The beautiful white elm, one of our most magnificent trees, has been wiped out over wide areas where these beetles, and the disease they bring, have spread.

The peculiar centipedelike engravings under the elm bark, made by the elm bark beetle larvae, show the actual territory covered by each larva as it wanders out from its central gallery to find more food in the cambium of the tree.

There are many other kinds of bark beetles (Scolytidae), including probably the largest number of dangerous tree pests in the world. The curious patterns made by some other bark beetle larvae under the bark of a Douglas fir in the West are shown in the accompanying photo. Bark becomes loose on a tree where this has happened and can be stripped off to expose the borings of the beetle larvae underneath. But only take off a little bit, as sometimes a tree can be saved even when it is being attacked by insect enemies. Each kind of bark beetle has a different kind of pattern it leaves under the bark, and experts can tell you the kind just from the design. It is enough for us to know that bark beetle larvae are doing this engraving and that it is harmful to the tree. If you find several trees so infested, please notify your nearest forestry station.

Notice the picture of the red turpentine beetles and their larvae and pupae uncovered when the bark is stripped off a tree these beetles are infesting. Grubs like these were once eaten by Indians, and I had some once when lost in the jungle of Panama and very hungry. They can sustain the life of a man lost and starving in the woods if he can put aside squeamishness about what to eat in favor of staying alive! Beetle grubs like these destroy the cambium, or life layer of the tree, and may encircle it, thus cutting off the flow of fluids up and down the trunk, and bringing death.

Pupae and eggs of many insects are found hanging in crevices of the bark, and under branches, twigs, and leaves of many trees (see photo of gypsy moths and their pupae). These are most easily found in winter when the leaves are stripped from the trees. If there are large groups of them, they tell us that either there has been a heavy infestation of these trees by harmful pests (if what we see are pupae), or that such an infestation is coming soon (if what we see are eggs). Eggs, being small, are sometimes hidden under the bark to protect them from enemies and the weather. In the spring they turn into larvae which either bore under the bark or climb out on the leaves to feed on them.

Tunnels and galleries of bark beetle larvae under Douglas fir bark.—*Photo courtesy American Forest Products Industries, Inc.*

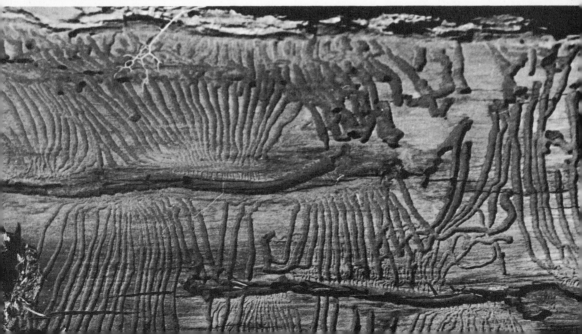

Red turpentine beetles and their galleries, pupae, and full-grown larvae between bark and wood.—*Photo courtesy U.S. Department of Agriculture.*

Gypsy moths and pupae on tree trunk.—*Photo courtesy U.S. Department of Agriculture.*

Gypsy moth caterpillars at work.—*Photo courtesy U.S. Department of Agriculture.*

Leaf Eaters

The gypsy moth caterpillars are among many kinds of insects, including plant lice, mealybugs, various plant bugs, katydids, and others, which voraciously feed on leaves. If we see leaves cut up, with large chunks taken out of them, we know that insects with chewing mouth parts, like the katydids and the caterpillars, have been working on them. Often these creatures cannot be seen in the daylight, because they hide when the sun is up, and come out at night to eat when they are less visible to their enemies. Trees dying from this cause are shown in the accompanying photo. If the leaves are not cut up, but discolored, then you know insects with sucking mouth parts, such as aphids, cicadas, plant bugs, leafhoppers, etc. have been sucking the juices out of them, and that is just as dangerous to the life of the tree as biting out pieces from the

Gypsy moth caterpillars have eaten all the leaves off of these trees, killing them if they are pines or hemlocks, killing deciduous trees after two such defoliations.—*Photo courtesy U.S. Department of Agriculture.*

leaves. Still a third way of attack on the leaves is perpetrated by the leaf miners, very tiny insect larvae that actually eat little tunnels through the leaves between the upper and lower surfaces, hiding in this way from their enemies. These little tunnels are seen as pale lines in the leaf's surface, often looking like a maze. But they kill the leaf as surely as the biting of caterpillars or the sucking of plant juices by plant lice. Death comes to the tree in time if these dangerous insects are not stopped.

Insect Population Control

The life in the forest can be thought of as a great circle. When the circle is in balance, the life of the forest is healthy and the forest grows, but, if the balance is upset, the trees begin to die and the forest may shrink till it is nothing. So the birds and insectivorous mammals, such as the moles, shrews, bats, and grasshopper mice, hunt constantly for insects, killing unfortunately the good as well as the bad, but helping to keep down the numbers of destructive pests. But the greatest curb on insects harmful to the forest is probably provided by other insects that attack them, such as the robber flies, the carnivorous wasps (hornets and yellow jackets in particular), the parasitic wasps, the ladybird beetles, the ground beetles, and so on. These enemies of the tree-killing insects, constantly hunting them or parasitizing them, keep them from producing the vast numbers that sometimes wipe out whole forests.

Tree Galls: Harmful or Not?

The galls that some insects produce on the branches and leaves of trees (see picture of cynipid galls) are often strange and interesting signs of insect work in the forest. Some become as large as baseballs. "Gall" is a name for any swelling found on a tree branch or leaf, produced by the insertion of something foreign under the surface that causes the place on the plant to swell in self-protection. Most of the gall insects literally sting the tree with the tips of their ovipositors, which bore holes into the leaves, bark, or twigs and deposit eggs. The tree swells up the part in answer to this sting and thereby furnishes the young larva that comes out of each egg a protective home and plenty of plant food. It is hard to know just how much harm to the tree is done by this. Many

Cynipid galls of cynipid gall wasp *(Callirhytis seminator)* on white oak. The galls at first contain larvae, then pupae, which emerge as adults in June.—*Photo courtesy U.S. Department of Agriculture.*

trees that are covered with one kind of gall or another appear to be perfectly healthy. After the larva has lived long enough inside the gall, eating the plant food provided for it there, it pupates and then later emerges from the pupa as an adult insect that cuts its way out of the gall. You can thus always tell an empty gall from one in use by observing the hole on the side of the gall where the insect comes out. Most tree galls are caused by various cynipid gall wasps, but gall midges form galls on willows. Both are very tiny creatures.

WHAT PLANTS DO TO EACH OTHER

Some plants are as great enemies of other plants as are the injurious insects. This is especially true of the fungi. But other plants appear to cooperate with each other, or, even in a sense, sacrifice themselves for the sake of other plants as we have seen in the case of the nurse or foster-mother trees (see Chapter 4). Once a climax forest is established (see Examples of Plant Succession in Chapter 6), plants seem to come into balance with one another for long periods of time and the struggle for existence is not so evident. For example, in a redwood forest, the great trees shade innumerable smaller plants possessing large, light-sensitive leaves that are especially adapted for this kind of environment, so that other plants that are light-loving are kept out. The young redwoods have little chance to start in these dark, shady places, but begin to sprout and reach up immediately wherever one of the giants has fallen, making a hole in the sky down which the rays of sunlight come to give life and growth to the young trees.

The greatest time of competition between trees is usually at the start of new growth, after an area has had the original forest cleared away by man or fire. At this time there is plenty of light at first for the new young trees, but, as they grow, they become more and more crowded together. Unless man comes and thins them out to help their growth, a deadly struggle sets in where accidents of soil and position and kind of tree allow some trees to outgrow others and eventually shade them out and kill them by superior growth. Once the large trees of a major forest have grown to a goodly height, this intense competition begins to fade away and the trees are in balance, as stated above.

The chart below shows some of the major effects plants have on plants and the signs you should watch for in the forest that tell of these things happening.

Plant Interactions

Signs of plant interaction	Plants that interact	Results
Ordinary vines climbing up over trees, bushes, etc. No sign of vines constricting trees.	Poison oak and ivy, virgin's bower, wild blackberry, English ivy, woodbine, wild cucumber, vine maple, etc.	These plants climb on many trees and large bushes, their leaves sometimes cutting off sunlight from the plants they climb on, but rarely do more than stunt their growth. Vines help themselves by climbing to light.
Strangling vines which actually constrict branches and trunks of trees.	Strangler fig vine of southern Florida.	This vine usually starts as a seed in the crotch of a tree, drops down a root to the ground, then twines tightly around the tree until it kills it and takes its place.

Plant Interactions (continued)

Signs of plant interaction	Plants that interact	Results
Parasitic vines and other tree parasites often not having connection with ground, but stealing food from host.	Dodder, a parasitic vine, and mistletoe, growing as parasite in top of tree.	These plants take sap from host tree to use for themselves and eventually may kill tree. Mistletoe is not completely parasitic, as it has green leaves; dodder leaves have no green.
Blighted and dying trees, often covered with black, rusty, or gray scales, but with no sign of insect work or large plant parasites.	Wood-destroying bracket fungus, chestnut-blight fungus, other tree-blight fungi, blister rusts, rusts, etc.	Trees are shriveled and killed in wholesale manner by these deadly fungi diseases. Bracket fungus sinks its mycelium (rootlike structures) deep into trees.
Trees overcrowding each other in young growth.	Most trees in young new forests.	Growth of all trees is limited by overcrowding, often producing scraggly appearance; weaker trees are gradually shaded out and die.
Trees fallen on other trees or shrubs.	Old, diseased, or fire-weakened trees.	Harm is caused when tree hits other trees and weakens their roots, or prevents sun from reaching leaves. Good is caused by letting in sunlight for new growth and by decay of tree, producing new soil.
Nurse or foster-mother trees that help young trees get started.	Aspens, jack pines, birches, hawthorns, scrub oaks, etc.	Young climax trees restore climax forest in time, but shade out and kill nurse trees.

Harmful Fungi

BRACKET FUNGUS   The accompanying photo shows a typical wood-destroying bracket fungus. The mycelium, consisting of rootlike, threadlike growths that descend from this fungus into the heart of the tree, takes nourishment away from the tree and eventually may kill it. Such bracket fungi are sad things to see, if we love trees, for they show that the tree has been wounded in some way at this point by a bird, insects, a falling tree, the wind breaking a branch, an animal, or a man using an axe or knife carelessly, and so forth. The fungi used the wound as an entrance to get in and attack the cambium. A tree so attacked will probably have its life greatly shortened, its wood ruined as potential lumber, and its possibility of falling down in some storm greatly enhanced. Bracket fungi on many trees in a forest are a sure sign of doom. You can help prevent the spread of this destruction by carrying a pail of semiliquid tar into a forest and plastering some on any wound you see in the bark, or, if a branch has broken, cutting off the break square with a saw, and coating the end with tar. Since the

Wood-destroying bracket fungus.—*Photo courtesy Ontario Department of Lands and Forests.*

spores of this and other fungi are in the very air, waiting for an opportunity to light on such a wound, openings that lead into the vital life of a tree cannot be covered too soon. You can, in truth, be a true guardian of the trees of our land if you undertake this job, and worthy, if other people would only realize it, of a medal of honor for life-saving, human as well as tree!

CHESTNUT TREE BLIGHT   The chestnut tree blight is an even more dangerous fungus. It almost completely wiped out one of the most magnificent forest trees in all

Dead Chestnut trees in Tennessee highlands, killed by chestnut blight disease.—*Photo courtesy Tennessee Department of Conservation.*

North America, the American chestnut, whose tasty nuts were once sold on many a midwestern street. Some of the trees that were blighted by the fungus are shown in the accompanying photo. This blight, a virulent fungus disease, is carried by the wind, and shows how some trees, even as some human beings who have no resistance to certain diseases (like the Indians encountering smallpox for the first time), can be wiped out wholesale by the coming of a new and terrible death. The wind-borne spores entered holes in the bark made by beetles, as well as other wounds, and quickly attacked the cambium in such a way as to destroy it. The great chestnut forests disappeared, but, for many years, the dead stumps were an ugly blot on eastern landscapes. A resistant form of the tree may eventually start bringing the chestnut forest back, but this is far in the future. Our country must be vigilant that other similar plant diseases will not come to destroy other of our beautiful trees.

Plant Parasites

Mistletoes are parasites that have pale green leaves so that they can manufacture their own plant food, but nevertheless depend on their host plants to supply them with water and minerals. Thus they are not as bad on a tree as the dodder vine, which does not have its own chlorophyll, and so completely parasitizes and often kills the tree. However, trees heavily infested with mistletoes are weakened by these parasites and may eventually die (see picture of mistletoes infesting oak trees). Seeds of mistletoe are carried by birds, who eat the berries but do not digest all of the seeds, which are dropped on other trees. In the deserts of the Southwest there are mistletoes that have edible berries, eaten by the Indians.

MAN: THE DESTROYER AND RENEWER

While the red man of old treated the forests and woods of America with reverence and respect, seeing in them the influence of the Great Spirit, the white man, unfor-

Mistletoes infesting oak trees in Santa Fe National Forest, New Mexico.—*Photo courtesy U.S. Forest Service.*

tunately, saw in trees either something to be destroyed to build a farm where the forest had been, or something to exploit as a producer of lumber and so also destroy. But man the destroyer in America is coming near the end of his rope, now that the great forests have shrunk to the point of danger to man himself. So man the renewer of life is, to our possible future honor, beginning to counter and even throw back the efforts of man the destroyer. It is sad, however, that man the destroyer did not realize much sooner the need to change his spots and create beauty instead of to annihilate it.

As we travel through the forests of America, we can gauge wherever we go the results of these two conflicting tendencies, one moment filled with sadness and anger where we see the foolish destructive tendency of mankind, another moment filled and inspired with joy when we see where man has taken after his Creator to bring back and protect beauty in woods and trees. The signs are all about us, and here is a chart of the more common ways in which man affects the woods.

Signs of Man in the Woods

Signs man leaves	Causes	Results
Wholesale cutting down of trees.	Lumbering for immediate profit, without thought of tomorrow.	Trees are wiped out of wide areas without efforts to replace them, so that erosion and waste are caused.
Rocks and gravel piled against trees.	Old stream beds being dredged up to find gold.	Trees are not only destroyed, but good soil is covered with sterile gravel.
Eroded cliffs and hills.	High-pressure hoses used in hydraulic gold-mining turned on the hillsides.	Erosion of good topsoil and tree destruction is terrible.
Widespread erosion near logging roads.	Bulldozing roads through woods with no attempt to grade properly for soil protection.	Erosion when rains come washes away tremendous quantities of topsoil, making renewal of the forest very difficult.
Highways, especially superhighways, too close to woods.	Planning by engineers who have no concept of forest values and so do not make allowances to guard and protect trees.	If highways are designed and engineered to avoid valuable forest land or at least protect as much as possible, damage is not too bad; otherwise they destroy beautiful landscape.
Cut-off hilltops and rock-filled valleys.	Strip mining of valuable ores by using enormous digging machines.	Beautiful forest and meadowland are inexcusably destroyed—a monument to utter selfishness!
Movement of logs out of forest by cable or helicopter.	New scientific methods of tree removal to prevent erosion.	Results are good, as long as log removal is coupled with systematic tree reproduction and conservation of forest. Erosion is prevented, as logging trucks are gone.

Signs of Man in the Woods (continued)

Signs man leaves	Causes	Results
Litter of wood chips and other organic debris spread over tree-cut land.	Large machines that cut up remaining branches and other debris into small parts in rotary blades and spew this organic mulch out over cut-over land by powerful blowers.	Soil is covered with protective layer that rots into the earth to produce better soil. Land is protected until trees can begin to grow.
Small trees planted in orderly rows in holes dug out and filled with mulch and fertilizer.	Forestry workers digging and planting by this method to produce new forests.	Results are good if proper shade is left nearby or other wise methods are used to protect and encourage growth of new forest.
Thinning of brush and trees and burning of diseased trees.	Forestry workers cutting out dangerous fire-producing brush and cutting and burning diseased trees.	Healthy growth of forest is encouraged and fire danger is cut down.
Strip and block cutting of trees.	Intention of wise lumber companies to minimize erosion.	This method also helps reseeding of cut areas; erosion is much less if logs are moved by cable or copter.
Mildly burnt area.	Forestry or park crews burning out underbrush.	If properly done, this greatly cuts fire hazards and encourages wildlife by producing food for deer, etc. It can be bad if young trees are killed.
Fires leaving vast blackened areas.	Careless campers, hunters, etc.	Terrible destruction of trees and soil is produced.

Man's Wasteful Practices

Never in the history of the world has man been so careless of natural resources as in America. Finding a vast wilderness land, prodigal with woods and forests and other natural beauties, minerals, and soils, the white people in America have been wasting it at a reckless pace for years. In Minnesota and Michigan, for example, careless lumberers and campers started fires in tinder-dry woods time and again that wiped out forests in 10,000-square-mile areas. Men of those days simply took it as part of the hazards of the game of making profits as fast as possible! Such incredible blindness to the destruction of one's own wealth and self-interest had to stop sometime, and the middle of the twentieth century has finally brought a rude awakening. That the awakening is still not deep or strong enough is shown by the fact that we still have too many careless campers and hunters, still far too many man-made fires, and too many fly-by-night lumber companies, simply out for the fast buck, continuing to operate in back areas of America, cutting down trees without regard for the future. I can see the results of such destruction within ten miles of my ranch right now!

GOLD DREDGING   We can still see in the West the results of gold dredging in destroyed forest and meadow (see picture), but fortunately this is outlawed now in most states. The typical dredger got the gold-bearing gravel dug up and run through his machine to extract gold, and then threw the gravel out of the way where it would not affect his operation. If it happened to smash down trees or destroy a beautiful meadowland, this was unimportant to him. Such gravel-spoiled areas may take centuries before they begin to return to forests.

SURFACE STRIP MINING   Similar to gold dredging is surface strip mining, something done extensively in West Virginia, but common in many other parts of America. It is actually worse than gold dredging or hydraulic mining, for such huge digging machines and earthmovers are used that whole mountaintops are cut off and then canyons and valleys filled with crushed rock, destroying any forests or woods that happen to be in the way. Perhaps no more ruthless and destructive method of exploiting the earth is in practice today. The excuse of better profits is utterly ridiculous when millions of Americans are being deprived of the beauty and interest, education and recreation that is in the forests and hills simply to make somebody rich! Such selfishness sometimes has no end until it is stopped by law.

HYDRAULIC MINING   Hydraulic mining was once common in various mining areas, but is now fortunately stopped by law. Huge streams of water were shot out of great fire hoses, propelled by powerful pumps, and used to wash down mountain- and hillsides to get at the gold or other metal ores underneath the soil and surface rock. The incredible erosion is pictured on p. 78, and still remains in many areas as a monument to man's greed and to the destruction of forests that are all but impossible to bring back to where they once were.

RUTHLESS LOGGING   The results of ruthless logging of mountainsides and the erosion caused by poorly constructed logging roads are shown on pp. 78-79. The signs of this are completely stripped hillsides, gullies of erosion beginning to form, and no sign of any attempt to save the land or replant the forests. Carelessness, selfishness, ignorance are written all over the face of this ruined skin of the earth. How the shades of the old Indians must weep!

Gold-dredged meadow near Minersville, Trinity County, California.—*Photo courtesy National Park Service.*

Cliffs eroded by hydraulic mining in the Sierras.—*Southern Pacific photo.*

Severe erosion and forest destruction by logging in Mendocino County, California.—*Photo courtesy Department of Forestry, University of California at Berkeley.*

Road being built through forest, destroying trees and setting up problems in erosion.—*Photo courtesy U.S. Forest Service.*

Unscrupulous logging in Mt. Hood National Forest in Oregon produced this scene of destruction.—*Photo courtesy Library of Congress.*

New Lumbering Ways That Save the Woods

In the darkest night there eventually comes light, and so it happened that light eventually came to the darkness of destruction that, for so long, foolishly swept over the forests of America. President Theodore Roosevelt, Gifford Pinchot, the great forester of the early nineteen hundreds, and others began to preach the doctrine of conservation instead of destruction. American foresters and lumbermen visited Europe and saw how Germany, Sweden, France, and other countries were carefully preserving the precious assets of forest land that men of those regions now realized were priceless!

Now, all over America, there are refreshing signs that both lumbermen and foresters are understanding that trees must be farmed rather than mined. It is not all this way yet, as private property owners still sell valuable woods to the ruthless destroyers, as well as to equally ruthless real estate land sharks who want to turn the land into suburbs regardless of the trees that are destroyed. But most of the

Douglas fir forest cut down in blocks to help reseeding and conservation.—*Photo courtesy U.S. Department of Agriculture.*

Alternate clear-strip cutting in spruce-fir forest, Colorado, helps forest conservation.—*Photo courtesy U.S. Department of Agriculture.*

great lumber companies have wisely begun to create tree farms where everything is done to cut down on erosion and bring back both the soil and the trees, and more and more landowners are beginning to see the long-time value of saving their trees and farming them cautiously, if at all.

One of the first signs of this change is the practice of cutting only certain sections of a forest and allowing the other parts to continue to grow, to protect the soil and hillsides from erosion and to produce the seeds for the new trees that are needed to replace those cut. This is shown in the pictures of block cutting and alternate clear-strip cutting of trees. Two other ideas have come into tree farming that are strictly for soil preservation and the stopping of erosion. One is the use of a powerful cable to carry logs away over the treetops instead of in trucks over the old-type logging roads that so terribly gouged and eroded the soil, or the equally wasteful way of dragging logs through the forest with a cable and winch. The cable in the picture is attached to

Skagit skycar carries log on cable high above trees by using cable hook operated by remote control.—*Photo courtesy American Forest Products Industries, Inc.*

tall poles, treetops, or high hillsides; then a trolley with a hook fastened to another cable carries each log out of the forest and to a place where it can be loaded without injuring the soil or the woods. The second way is to use a helicopter, with a steel cable and hooks hanging below to lift and carry logs out of the forest.

Science and intelligence combined with the real human urge of sensitive people to beautify the earth may eventually overcome man's urge to destroy and exploit the natural world for the sake of money. There are some things infinitely more valuable than money, and a beautiful forest or wood is one of them.

REFORESTATION   So today, into the burnt-over and cut-over forests go Forest Service crews and wise lumbermen to plant new trees to take the place of the burnt or cut ones (see the picture of a Forest Service crew in action). The men in the picture have come in after the ground has had a few years of the growth of grass and herbs to help renew the soil. With mattocks they dig holes in the earth and plant a young seedling ponderosa pine in each hole. Often fertilizer and mulch is put into the hole with the dirt to help the young tree grow. When rains come the seedling will begin to stretch down its roots and lift up its tiny branches to the sky, and a new forest will be on its way!

When fire has scorched the soil so much that little humus remains, planes come flying low and drop grass seed over the land. This grass, of a special kind designed to bind and rebuild the soil by adding organic matter to it until it is ready for the first young trees, grows quickly and thickly with the coming of the first rains. Later herbs come too and then bushes—each one of the steps in the journey back to the ancient owners of the land, the great trees of the climax forest (see Examples of Plant Succession in Chapter 6).

The greatest danger to the renewal of life on burnt or cut ground, as the good forester well knows, is the situation on hillsides, especially steep ones, where erosion caused by heavy rainfall or runoff from melting snow may not only destroy the plant life on the hillside, but also trees lower down that are killed by too much soil being washed down upon them (see Ruinous Torrential Rain at the end of Chapter 2). Not only is the sowing of grass and the adding of mulch required in such places, but also small rush and log dams may be needed where gullies are getting ready to start on the hills. Contour plowing to form level channels along the sides of the hills is often needed to carry the water of rainfall and melting snow along the slope instead of down it.

Forest Service crew planting young ponderosa pines in burned-over area of Apache National Forest, Arizona.—*Photo courtesy U.S. Forest Service.*

Thinning out brush and diseased trees to help healthy growth of forest.—*Photo courtesy Library of Congress.*

Wherever we see the signs in the woods of these constructive works of man we know that he is acting wisely and working to bring back the beauty of the land and strengthen the earth's skin. One day in such places the wind will sing in the pines again or sigh through the hemlocks and the firs.

WEEDING OUT DISEASED PLANTS   We can realize now how diseased trees and trees attacked by insects act as centers from which these diseases and harmful insects move out into surrounding forest areas with their destruction. Sometimes, as in the Far West, bushes like the wild gooseberry act as hosts to diseases which the larger trees catch. When man thins out this kind of brush and all diseased trees by cutting them down and then piling those that have no commercial value for burning, he is protecting the forest from contamination (see photo). The theory is that if the diseased trees and bushes are wiped out, the pests that cause these conditions will be largely destroyed also and the healthy trees will be better able to resist them. How

Eighteen-year-old pine plantation in Madison County, Alabama, showing healthy growth of man-planted forest.—*Photo courtesy Tennessee Valley Authority.*

successful this is has not yet been thoroughly determined in all areas, though the eradication of diseased gooseberry bushes in the West to protect the pines has had good results.

The eighteen-year-old pine plantation in the picture shows orderly rows of young pines, properly spaced for light and air, and showing healthy signs of building a future mature forest. Notice the thick layer of tree needles, broken branches, and other forest trash covering the ground below the trees. This forms a mulch that strengthens the resistance of the soil to erosion and protects it from losing moisture, though large dead branches may form a fire danger. If no fire comes, both moisture and soil are conserved and the trash gradually decays into fine humus mixed through the soil by the falling of rain. Another sign to notice in this picture is how the lower branches of these pines are dying because they are below the area where enough sunlight comes through the needles of the higher branches to make live pine needles possible. These dead and brittle limbs are often broken off by the foresters to encourage the growth of more decaying mulch on the forest floor and to cut down on the danger of ground fires sweeping up the trunks and forming a crown fire. Eventually the tree may grow straight up without a branch for fifty feet or more, the sure sign of a good timber tree, whose food-producing branches are found only high up in the golden sunlight of the forest tops.

A healthy yellow poplar tree (also called tulip tree and other names), such as the one shown in the photograph, is a delight to the eyes when its large waxy yellow flowers come into bloom in the springtime and set the forest alight with golden spots of glory. Dedicated tree farmers, like the owner of the tree in the picture, not only love trees, but plan, grow, and harvest their woods with the greatest wisdom and care to make sure that the complete resurrection and renewal of the forest is carried out at all times, even as the carefully selected and marked mature trees are thinned out and hauled away to be sold as lumber. What a far cry is this harmony with nature and understanding of the need for balance in the circle of life from the profit- and destruction-mad lumbering outfits of yore who went into the wilderness with no more appreciation of the many more real values of what they were wiping out than a mosquito has of a beautiful sunset!

Tree-farmer Mrs. Dorsey Brown admires a yellow poplar bloom on her 750-acre Kentucky tree farm.—*Photo courtesy American Forest Products Industries, Inc.*

PLANTS THAT FEED WILDLIFE

In the woods we are constantly seeing animals, birds, insects, and other creatures feeding on the leaves, bark, roots, fruits, bulbs, and seeds of plants, or finding the results of their feeding. Such things are part of the signs seen in the woods that help us read them. It is unfortunate that we cannot be confident that just because an animal or bird has eaten some wild fruit, seed, or root that we can eat it also. Some such foods have poisons or distasteful products in them that the bird or animal seems to be able to handle without being hurt, while we may find them dangerous. The accompanying chart shows a few of the many wild plants that are edible for both animals and man. See Selected References for the names of books on this subject.

Whipple yucca in blossom in California chaparral. Its fruit is eaten by both animals and man.—*Photo courtesy U.S. Forest Service.*

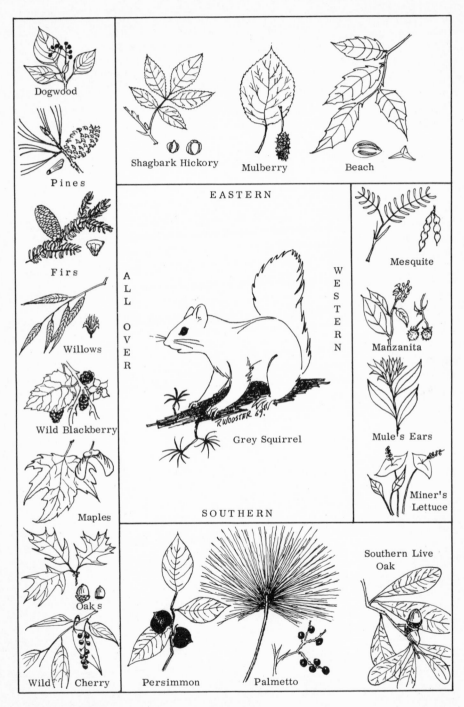

Dogwood

Pines

Firs

Willows

Wild Blackberry

Maples

Oaks

Wild Cherry

Shagbark Hickory

Mulberry

Beach

EASTERN

ALL OVER

WESTERN

Mesquite

Manzanita

Mule's Ears

Miner's Lettuce

Grey Squirrel

R WOOSTER 69.

SOUTHERN

Persimmon

Palmetto

Southern Live Oak

Edible Plants

These plants are used principally by wildlife, but most of them are also edible by man (see also chart, Principal Feeders on Popular Wild Food Plants, on pp. 86-87).

Since the white man came to America tremendous changes have happened to the wildlife of this continent. Some species, like the trumpeter swan, the passenger pigeon and the buffalo, have been completely or nearly wiped out by man. But others, such as the coyote, opossum, raccoon, California quail, bluebird, bobwhite, and so forth, have adapted themselves to man's coming and actually increased in number and range. One of the things that has helped some animals is the opening up of the dense forests to light and the creation of more open-type woods, such as shown in the woodlot picture under Woodlots of Eastern and Midwestern Farms in Chapter 8. Increased agriculture and spread of weeds have helped spread some species like crows, pocket gophers, starlings, and English sparrows.

Animals and birds are usually associated with special plant foods that they crave more than others and so leave signs of their passing by feeding on them. Some creatures are even named after the plant they feed on, as, for example, the cedar waxwings, because they feed so much on cedar or juniper berries, and the pinyon jays, whose flocks love to eat the pinyon pine nuts of the intermountain west. The chart below shows some of the principal trees and plants and the common wild animals and birds that feed on them so you can watch for these in the woods.

Principal Feeders on Popular Wild Food Plants

Plants	Parts of plants eaten	Principal animal feeders	Principal bird feeders
pines	nuts	chipmunks, tree squirrels	grouse, jays, grosbeaks, nuthatches, crossbills, nutcrackers, wild turkeys
pines	bark	deer, porcupines	
pines	twigs	deer	
pines	foliage	deer	grouse, jays, grosbeaks, nuthatches, crossbills, nutcrackers, wild turkeys
firs	leaves and twigs	deer, moose	
firs	seeds	chickarees, porcupines	grouse, chickadees, nutcrackers
firs	bark	chickarees, porcupines	
junipers and cedars	fruits	deer, antelopes, white-footed and pocket mice	pinyon jays, grosbeaks, waxwings, purple finches, solitaires
hickories and pecans	nuts	tree squirrels, chipmunks, deer, beavers, hares	wood ducks, grosbeaks, woodpeckers, grouse, prairie chickens, quail
aspens and poplars	buds, catkins, and foliage	deer, moose, beavers, hares	grouse, prairie chickens, quail
aspens and poplars	bark	beavers	
willows	bark, buds, and twigs	beavers, hares, deer, moose	grouse

Principal Feeders on Popular Wild Food Plants (continued)

Plants	Parts of plants eaten	Principal animal feeders	Principal bird feeders
hazelnuts	buds, nuts, twigs	beavers, hares, chipmunks	grouse
beeches	nuts and buds	bears, porcupines, tree squirrels	grouse, jays, titmice
oaks	acorns and buds	bears, raccoons, tree squirrels, deer, peccaries	wood ducks, ruffed grouse, pigeons, prairie chickens, quail
oaks	twigs and foliage	deer, peccaries	
black-berries	fruit	marmots, chipmunks, cottontails, bears	grouse, pheasants, prairie chickens, grosbeaks, jays, tanagers
wild cherries	fruit, buds	bears, cottontails, chip-munks, jackrabbits	grouse, grosbeaks, robins, thrushes, waxwings, wood-peckers
mesquites	seeds	skunks, pocket mice, kan-garoo rats, wood rats	desert quail
mesquites	bark and leaves	jackrabbits	
sumacs	foliage	rabbits, deer	
sumacs	fruit	rabbits, deer, chipmunks	grouse, wild turkeys, starlings
poison ivy and oak	foliage	pocket mice	
poison ivy and oak	seeds	pocket mice	flickers, kinglets, sapsuckers, thrashers, thrushes, wren-tits
maples	seeds, foliage	porcupines, tree squirrels, chipmunks, wood rats, deer	grouse, grosbeaks, bob-whites
maples	sap	bears, deer, squirrels	sapsuckers
dogwoods	foliage	rabbits, deer	
dogwoods	fruit	rabbits, deer, chipmunks	grouse, pigeons, cardinals, grosbeaks, robins, thrushes, waxwings

CHAPTER SIX

Appreciating Nature's Survival Scheme

NORTH AMERICA HAS one of the richest floras of the world, rich in interesting and varied plant communities, and rich in the beauty and grandeur of its trees. We possess the greatest trees on earth, the redwoods and the giant sequoias; the oldest, the bristlecone pines; and some of the most beautiful, like white elm, white oak, sugar maple, and paper birch. But this very richness has made our forests the target for two centuries of the exploiter and destroyer. Ruthless man cuts down for instant profit, with no thought of tomorrow, and has carelessly let the forests of millions of acres burn or be totally cut because he dreams they are endless. But tomorrow has now come and with it the awakening. We find ourselves with a steadily increasing population in a land which once raised the spires of mighty trees to cover over half of our country, and now they are cut down to about one-fifth of our space. The time has come to reverse the process and bring back more trees to fill our lives with interest and joy, comfort and knowledge and spirit.

PLANT COMMUNITIES

From east to west and north to south the trees write the stories of their lives in living plant communities that grow or decrease in size and richness on the basis of what happens to their soil, their climate, and the actions of man and fire, insects and disease. We have seen some of the effects of these things on them, but let us look now at the plant communities as living entities, each like a city of men, with its diverse races and kinds, influencing and being influenced by each other. We no longer have as much as we used to of the great climax forest communities of early America that stretched for hundreds and sometimes thousands of miles with scarcely a change in general appearance. Instead, primarily because of the actions of man and fire, we have many lesser communities interspersed through the great communities or even taking their places over wide areas. But even these lesser communities of plants have their interesting features that we will learn about in the pages that follow.

It will help in learning to know these many beautiful plant communities, these cities of the green world, to think of each as having different layers and groups of plants fitted for different capacities and functions. Thus we can think of a woodland or forest, such as the oak woodland of California, or the great spruce-fir forests of Canada, as each having trees and plants in the following categories:

Citizens of Plant Communities

TREES   (1) Climax trees are those that rise to overshadow other trees and take their places in time. These make up the top story of all climax forests. (2) Secondary trees are those that have adapted themselves to living among the primary climax trees, but usually at a lower level. (3) Nurse trees are those that move in wherever the climax trees are destroyed so that the sunlight is let into the forest. These nurse trees can grow in poorer soil than the climax trees, but, as they rebuild the soil, they protect the nurslings of the climax trees that eventually start growing again by shading them. They are, if fire or tree-cutting is not repeated, replaced by the climax trees growing above them and shading them out.

SHRUBS AND VINES   (1) Climax shrubs are those that have adapted themselves to living under the deep shade of the climax trees by developing large, light-seeking leaves. They usually form a lower story of the forest, just above the grasses and the herbs. (2) Vines are those plants that have learned to climb up other shrubs and trees to find light. (3) Adventitious shrubs or bushes are those that come in to grow quickly where the great trees have fallen or have been burnt away. Even a small open space made by one large tree falling may have these shrubs temporarily. They help rebuild the soil after fire or erosion following tree-cutting, but they die when the great trees grow back again, because their leaves are too small for them to stand the shade.

HERBS, FERNS, AND GRASSES   (1) Climax herbs, ferns and grasses are those that are adapted, usually by large leaves, to living under the canopy of a climax forest. Most grasses cannot stand the shade, but some forests, such as the ponderosa pine forests of the West, have trees wide enough apart and letting in enough light for grasses to grow underneath them. (2) Adventitious herbs, ferns and grasses are those that cannot stand shade, but can grow up quickly on poor soil, ruined by fire or erosion, wherever the climax trees have been cut or burnt down. They act to rebuild the soil so that shrubs and then small trees, like the nurse trees, can begin to grow too.

OTHER PLANTS   These include mosses, liverworts, and fungi, which help in the rebuilding of soil and form usually the lowest story of the forest.

Some of these different types of plants are mentioned in the pages that follow so that reading the categories of plants listed above will help you understand them and see their signs in the forest. But it is impossible in the space allowed in this book to tell you something about more than a few of these many species and list some others that need mentioning. Nevertheless, the most important species will be touched upon and you will be given a good start.

THE MARCHING ARMIES OF PLANT SUCCESSION

Plant succession has already been mentioned in earlier parts of this book, and it is an important part of the everyday picture of plant communities in America, forming interesting signs that help you read the woods. It is indeed like watching marching armies of plants, for each of the several plant communities that make up a plant succession is like an army marching into enemy territory and seeking to put that territory to its own use.

A climatic region and particular kinds of soils, as well as mountains, plateaus, and hills, usually set up the conditions in which a type of climax forest can grow. Man, of course, can upset the balance of nature by his fires and cutting so that climax forests are supplanted over wide areas by secondary forests, and sometimes man's continued actions keep these forests in control and prevent the climax forests from coming back.

Examples of Plant Succession

CALIFORNIA'S REDWOOD FOREST   Let us examine a particular climax forest and how it takes over. On the northwest coast of California is the famous redwood forest, a true climax forest that once occupied at least twice the area it covers now. The climate includes the following: about 30 to 90 inches of rain a year, mainly in the winter and spring; an average of well over 300 frostfree days; cool but rarely cold winters; summers warm, but with numerous days in which fog comes in from the ocean, especially in the mornings. The soil overlays mainly granite or volcanic rocks and tends to be acidic rather than alkaline. The forest usually lies back of the immediate seacoast behind the hills or in canyons to avoid the sea winds.

Here then are the stages of what is called *primary plant succession* leading up to the climax redwood forest in a climate and area such as that described above.

1. Lichens and mosses growing on what was bare rock (see Soil in the Making in Chapter 3).
2. Liverworts, ferns, and small herbs (see Soil in the Making in Chapter 3).
3. Grasses and larger herbs. Fireweed is one of the principal herbs, especially if the land has recently been burnt over (see Quick-growing Weeds in Chapter 4).
4. Bushes, including thimbleberries, blackberries, wild lilac, coyote brush, etc.
5. Small to medium-sized deciduous trees: alders, box elders, buckeyes, live oaks, laurels, madrones, tanbark oaks, etc.
6. Lesser conifers, mainly Douglas firs.
7. Climax forest: redwoods above, with huckleberry bushes, and large-leaved herbs, mainly redwood sorrel and sword ferns, below. Tanbark oaks, vine maples, madrones, box elders, Douglas firs, and California laurels are secondary and fringe trees around the edge of this forest or wherever some light penetrates.

Secondary Plant Succession

Succession is so important a part of our wilderness scene and is so widespread in all plant communities that we cannot read the woods completely without looking for

Secondary Plant Succession in a Northeastern Forest

This is almost identical with plant succession in subalpine forest of the Rocky Mountains. From top to bottom, four stages are shown: (1) In first stage, a fierce crown forest fire has destroyed all tree life, leaving only a few burnt stubs, but flowers and grasses are beginning to spring up. (2) Second stage shows the coming of bushes like wild blackberry, ninebark, and black huckleberry. (3) Third stage sees growth of small, fast-growing trees like aspens (lighter-colored) and canoe birches, which act as nurse trees, giving necessary shade to slower-growing balsam firs and white and black spruces. (4) Fourth stage is return to climax forest in the form of mature balsam firs, white and black spruces, and an occasional large canoe birch.

signs of it. The two major kinds of plant succession are primary succession, which we have already examined, and secondary succession. Secondary succession is caused by the returning to climax forest of an area partially destroyed by fire, cutting, storm, or the like. In this case, the soil is not completely destroyed, though it may be severely damaged. Larger plants than the tiny ones that start plant growth and soil on a rock (described under Soil in the Making in Chapter 3) are able to start up soon after the destruction is over. Since secondary succession is the type we are most likely to see, typical examples of this kind of succession are shown in the chart below.

Some Common Secondary Plant Successions in America

Community after severe burn or flood	Second community	Third community	Climax community
Sedge grass and sphagnum moss, if in a bog area.	Fireweed, grasses, other herbs.	Alders, aspens, willows, mountain ash, raspberries, etc.	Balsam fir, white spruce, tamarack (much of Canada and N.E. edge of U.S.).
Fireweed, grass, and other herbs, if in dry area.	Alder, aspens, willows, red raspberry.	Paper birch, arborvitae, tamarack.	Balsam fir, white spruce, tamarack (same area as above).
Fireweed, grass, and other herbs.	Alders, aspens, willows, red raspberry.	Jack pine, paper birch, balsam poplar.	White pine and red pine (S.E. Canada and Minnesota to Maine).
Floating leaved plants, such as water purslane, water speedwell, etc.	Bulrushes, blazing star, loosestrife, water hemlock, etc.	Pitcher plant, sundew, cranberry, leatherleaf, bog rosemary, poison sumac, etc.	Tamarack, swamp cedar, black ash, black spruce, sugar maple, etc. (bogs and swamps of N.E. U.S.).
Fireweed, brambles, grasses, and herbs.	Bushes such as fire cherry, mountain maple, chokecherry, staghorn sumac, etc.	Mountain ash, rowan tree, sweet birch, and other small trees. Rhododendrons.	Red, silver, and sugar maples; oaks, yellow birch, beech, hemlocks, tulip tree, etc. (Appalachian deciduous forest).
Fireweed, grasses, herbs, etc.	Fire cherry, chokecherry, and other bushes.	Dogwood, witch hazel, and other small trees.	Birch-maple, beech-hemlock forest of middle northern states.
Grasses and herbs like trailing arbutus, wintergreen, etc.	Black haw, mountain laurel, red haw, crabapple, wild plums, etc.	Trembling aspen and jack pine in North; dogwoods, hawthorns, etc. in South.	Hickories, oaks, beech, sugar and silver maples, linden, ash, birches (central deciduous forest).
Grasses, sedges, cattails, small herbs.	Chokecherry, poison sumac, and other small bushes.	Sandbar and black willows, box elder, slash pine, overcup oak, and other small trees.	Sycamore, river birch, sweet gum, swamp chestnut oak, water oak, cottonwood, tulip tree, black willow, etc. (southern river bottom forest).

Some Common Secondary Plant Successions in America (continued)

Community after severe burn or flood	Second community	Third community	Climax community
Grasses, herbs.	Mountain mahogany, serviceberry, snowberry, etc.	Quaking aspen, lodgepole pine.	Douglas fir and Colorado blue spruce. Douglas fir forest in southern Rockies.
Grasses, herbs.	Sagebrush, bitterbrush, squawbush, scrub oak, etc.	Juniper, pinyon pine	Ponderosa pine forest in Rockies. Ponderosa pine, white fir.
Grasses, herbs.	Manzanita, sagebrush, wild lilac.	Black oak, dogwood, etc.	Ponderosa and sugar pines, white fir, incense cedar (Sierras).
Grasses, fireweed, and other herbs.	Alders, vine maple, willows, wild lilacs, thimbleberries, serviceberries, etc.	Cascara buckthorn, crabapple, Oregon ash, dogwood, mountain maple.	Douglas fir, western hemlock, grand fir (Douglas fir forest of Pacific Northwest).

CHAPTER SEVEN

Reading Signposts
in Evergreen Forests

Eastern White Pine

Eastern Hemlock

THE TREMENDOUS CHANGES brought by fire and lumbering over the past two hundred years have inevitably radically changed the appearances of many forests. Our tree sizes in the East now average much smaller than a hundred years ago, with comparatively few trees over a hundred feet in height. And there is a great change in the composition of the forests.

Forests in the old days mostly kept to themselves, like jealous nations, conifers with conifers, deciduous trees with deciduous trees, mostly because the conifers did not like the more acid soil where the deciduous trees grew. Exceptions to this rule were and are the white pine and eastern hemlock in the North, and the bald cypress and loblolly pine in the South, all four becoming adapted over a long period to living among the hardwoods. But the white man's smashing impact on the plants of North America so upset the balance that now we are finding more and more conifers and deciduous trees mixing together. Part of this is due, of course, to the fact that many more of our forests today are in different stages of succession with fewer true climax forests. In this bewildering mixture and change it seems as though certain advanced-type or adventurous trees—like the members of the rose family, such as the hawthorns, ashes, wild cherries, and wild plums, and similar members of the heath and dogwood families—are learning how to move into and take over many new habitats. Some of the conifers, including the jack pine, the Virginia or scrub pine, and the junipers of the West are doing the same thing.

CONIFEROUS FORESTS EAST OF THE ROCKIES

In the long ago, when the white people first landed on the eastern shore of North America, magnificent forests of virgin timber stretched for thousands of miles in the area east of the Rockies. Now any such forest is lucky if it occupies a hundred miles. It is fortunate indeed, though, that many trees seem to have a wonderful resilience in rebounding from the time of great destruction that swept our country from about 1800 to 1920, and here and there signs of the rebuilding of our forests are showing. Hopefully soon we will realize our priceless heritage and save and increase it as the Europeans are doing.

Paper Birch

The paper birch (see photo), from which the Indian and the American woodsman stripped the fine, light, firm bark to make the incredibly swift birch-bark canoes, is found over most of the Northeast. It is one tree that has withstood the ravages of the white man and even rebounded back in a profusion it did not have before. How glad we can be that this marvelous tree, gleaming in its white beauty, usually attractively marked with brown lenticels, stands before us in all this vast region of the north woods as a reminder of the glories of the past. Because it has an affinity for conifers and likes growing on the same kind of neutral soil, it is found constantly around their fringes and even marches with its boon companions, the balsam fir and the arborvitae, down to the clear, cold northern streams and lakes where it can throw its beautiful reflection on the crystal waters.

Arborvitae

NORTHERN SPRUCE-FIR FOREST

The northern spruce-fir forest originally covered the northern half of the northeastern tier of states west to Minnesota, most of northeastern Canada, and western Canada from the northern border of the Great Plains to the beginning of the Barren Lands. However, in modern times it has shrunk to strips in most of its former southern range, with the bulk of the forest now lying in central north Canada. In the United States white pine and red pine first took its place, and later jack pine, canoe birch, aspen, etc.

Three things make this true north woods forest, made up mainly of white spruce and balsam fir, but with many paper birches fringing the conifers, something to stand out forever in your memory once you have met it (see photo).

Red Pine

Paper birches at Winter Harbor, Maine.—*Photo courtesy Library of Congress.*

Balsam Fir

White Spruce

Black Spruce

As you enter its fringe, the first thing that strikes you is its smell. How can I describe it? Spicy, delectable, fragrant, pungent? It is all these things and more, perhaps most of all the scent of balsam fir that means the very essence of wilderness, purity, beauty, silence, or the whisper of wind and waters. To sleep on a fir bough bed with a balsam needle pillow is to nestle in the arms of a loving spirit, protected, invigorated, lulled, swept-over with waves of blessed fragrance. It is the balsam fir indeed that emits this scent, a scent that strangely dies away in your nostrils after a few weeks in the wilderness, but which lingers forever in your inner mind.

The second thing becomes apparent as you step beyond the outer fringe of the forest and in toward its mysterious center. The trees here—the white and black spruces, the balsam firs, the occasional tamarack and arborvitae—are thick-needled and dark with the feeling of night. Their spires rise above you a hundred feet or more, the branches forming shielding umbrellas that cut out the sunlight, and so you walk beneath them in seeming eternal shade as long as they are close together. Here and there, where a coniferous tree has died and fallen, swept down by the wind, a paper birch or two seems to spring up suddenly to dazzle your eyes with its snowy bark, its rustling, laughing, young green, dancing leaves, glistening with light, so different from the still and solemn needles of the great conifers; and the sun breaks through to relieve the gloom.

No wonder these great, grim, dark forests of the North frightened the first white colonists that came to America so that they usually left them strictly alone, realizing that eyes could watch them unseen from those dark depths. Even today the city man cannot walk among these trees without becoming quickly uneasy and with a well-founded fear that he might get lost. But, to those who get to know them, fear soon goes and something soothing and sacred replaces it.

And this is the third thing about this forest: the silence that strikes you when you are far within it, for, like most great coniferous forests, the trees are not too attractive to bird and animal or even insect life. The occasional songs or calls that do come—a hermit thrush spiraling notes of utter beauty through the shadows, the twittering or clicking of slate-colored juncos, the clear "tee-tee-too" whistle of a pine grosbeak—only accentuate the strange and brooding stillness, and there are long periods near midday when no sound comes at all

Highland white spruce and balsam fir near Gay, Keweenaw County, Michigan.— Photo courtesy U.S. Forest Service.

save a deep breathing of the wind high among the needles. And it is at such times that civilized man may be tested and found wanting, for he must rise above his momentary fear and depression of the spirit, and realize he is standing in a presence more meaningful and tremendous by far than anything found in the land of steel, brick, glass, and machines whence he came.

Like all forests, it may have, if the upper canopy is not too thick and dark, its layers or stories of plants. At the top stand the great conifers. Next come the few birches, paper and yellow, forming an occasional first understory. Below this appears a second understory of bushes, such as the hobblebush, northern wild raisin, and sweet viburnum. Still lower are the herbs, such as asters, oxalis, yellow clintonia, and wild sarsaparilla, but lowest of all are the mushrooms and moss.

Jack Pine

THE GREAT LAKES AND CENTRAL NEW ENGLAND CONIFEROUS FORESTS

Though stretches of the white spruce-balsam fir forest of the North are also found in areas around the upper parts of the Great Lakes and northern New England and New York, the main coniferous forest of this area is made up of pines. In the old days it was dominated by white pine (see photo of eastern white pine grove), with the red pine as secondary, but more than a century of destructive lumbering, combined with carelessly set but vastly destructive fires, have wiped out most of the virgin forests of red and white pine in the area. Though these pines are gradually coming back here and there and mixing in with other trees, much of the area is still in the process of secondary succession, in which the jack pine has become the temporarily dominant tree (see photo), though, in boggy areas of northern Minnesota and elsewhere, there are wide areas dominated by tamarack forests. These also, like the jack pine, are secondary and

Tamarack

Eastern white pine grove.—*Photo courtesy U.S. Department of Agriculture.*

Seventy-year-old stand of jack pines with young balsam firs below.—*Photo courtesy U.S. Forest Service.*

Tamarack

White Spruce

Black Spruce

nurse trees, moving in and taking over in places like the wet bogs where conditions are not yet ripe for the white and red pines or the northern spruce-fir forest.

Tamaracks are one of the two conifers in North America (the other is the bald cypress of the southern swamps) that lose their leaves in winter. Both apparently do so because of the extreme lack of oxygen in the decaying matter and mud found in the bogs and swamps about their roots. Such trees must bring oxygen down to their roots from the leaves, and the leaves are only able to do this during the warm season of the year. The tamaracks are among the most beautiful trees in spring and summer, when they are covered with an almost ethereal halo of light green needles, but become the most ugly of trees during the winter when the leaves are gone.

Though the red and white pines appear like climax trees, it is possible that they are actually a subclimax of long duration, forming a transitional area between the main coniferous forest on the north and the beginning of the main deciduous forest on the south. The transitional nature of the white pine is shown by its ability to live among both deciduous trees and as a part of the climax forests of spruce and balsam fir.

Where the land has been greatly impaired by either fire or overcutting by lumbermen, the soil is often not capable of raising the main conifers, and here the jack pine takes over because of its ability to grow in poor soil. The paper and yellow birches, and the quaking aspen are two other types of trees that also can move into sunlit open spaces where the land has been spoiled by fire or overcutting and grow into nurse trees. All four of these species not only build up the soil by dropping leaves and dead limbs upon it, but create the shade eventually needed to shelter the young white and red pines, balsam firs, and white and black spruces (see photo of White Mountains scene). The jack pine shows its nature by being a short-lived, poor-wooded, and often twisted tree, capable only of filling in for a time before the great trees take over, though on rocky and very dry soil it may repeat itself for generations.

How then can we know the characteristics and the feeling of these rather crazily mixed forests that have taken over from the great white pine and red pine stands of the pioneers? We can say that mainly and obviously these forests constitute a border country in many ways, a land of quiet warfare between the great conifers of the North and the marvelously adaptive and lively-appearing deciduous trees of the South. Thus, in one area an arm of the forest may be filled with the deep shade and gloom of the spruce-fir climax, while another stretch nearby has the yellow green, flashing needles of the tamarack bog forests, where the shining, rime-coated needles are like Saint Elmo's fire, carrying the sunlight with them right down to the boggy soil beneath which lie those strange fiberlike roots that were used by the Indians both to bind together birchbark canoes and to heal the wounds of war and the hunt. Over in still another place, where the soil is rich but not too damp, a clump of white pines shows us where the fine straight trunks are reaching even higher in an attempt to eventually top two hundred feet as their ancestors did in the long ago. Under such grand trees the wind in the needles has a clear, deep sound, unlike the whisper it makes in the tens of thousands of acres of scrub jack pines that stretch away to the horizon, usurping much of the land the white pine once owned.

Eastern Hemlock

But representatives of the deciduous forest stretch up into this region also, especially, of course, the canoe birch and the quaking aspen, both white-clad nurses of the great conifers. Then there is also the flame of red maple and the stately beauty of the sugar maple, both with hidden treasures of sweets. Into the southern edge of this region troop the yellow birch, the hickory, and even an occasional oak and basswood, while the arborvitae (a cedar), the widespread eastern hemlock, and the common juniper are other conifers that grace this mixed forest and woodland. Light and dark, green and yellow, brown and crimson, the forest is a mosaic of interest and beauty.

Arborvitae

ACADIAN-APPALACHIAN CONIFEROUS AND MIXED CONIFEROUS-HARDWOOD FORESTS

On the highest mountains of New England and right down the highest rim of the Appalachians clear to western North Carolina in the Southeast runs the same kind of forest found in northern Canada, the spruce-fir forest, but with some minor differences. The white spruce of the North fades away in northern New England and is replaced all through the mountains to the south by the red spruce.

Red Spruce

Scene in the White Mountains of New Hampshire. Dark trees are red spruce and balsam fir, plus a few red and white pines and eastern hemlocks. Light-colored trees are mainly aspens, maples and birches.—*Photo by Eric M. Sanford. Courtesy Alpha Photo Associates, Inc., 200 W. 57th St., New York, N.Y. 10019.*

Headwaters of Tellico River, Cherokee National Forest, Tennessee, with red and white pines, eastern hemlocks, southern balsam firs, maples, ashes, rhododendrons, red spruces, etc.—*Photo courtesy U.S. Forest Service.*

Eastern Hemlock

Eastern White Pine

Also, though the balsam fir extends south as far as western Virginia, it is replaced to the south of that by the southern balsam fir. But the appearance of these dark forests is almost exactly the same as their great cousins in the North (see photo of scene in Cherokee National Forest). Once again you meet the gloom and mystery within those ranks, smell the spicy odors of balsam, and feel the wonderful, but, to some people, frightening silence. The frequent rains and mists of these summits, probably outnumbering the snows, make for a feeling of dampness and hoary age that is accentuated by the deep green carpet of ferns, mosses, and lichens that cover the ground and the strange, stringy moss that often hangs like prophets' beards from many a dead branch.

The photo of the White Mountains scene earlier in this chapter shows how the deciduous forest invades the coniferous forest where it has been burned or overcut. The dark-colored trees of this high New England forest are instantly recognized by their spirelike shape as mainly red spruces and balsam firs, but the light-colored foliage shows considerable invasion by yellow, gray, and paper birches, and probably also quaking aspens, willows, and some maples. This invasion of succession-type trees will eventually, if fire or man do not interfere, be replaced by the complete climax spruce-fir forest of old. In the fall, though, the reds, yellows, and oranges of the maples, birches, and other deciduous trees flame to the sky, adding a beauty of quivering leaves and a singing that the coniferous forest can never equal.

EASTERN AND MIDWESTERN MIXED DECIDUOUS AND CONIFEROUS FORESTS

Red Pine

In this forest the deciduous trees usually outnumber the coniferous trees, and most of the coniferous trees are of two species, the eastern hemlock or the less numerous white pine, both of which are conifers that have apparently learned how to adapt themselves to the more acid deciduous forest soils. Most typical of this kind of forest is what is called the birch-beech-maple-hemlock complex. The dominant trees are eastern hemlock, the sugar and red maples, the yellow and cherry birches, and the beech (see photo of stand in Pennsylvania). Less frequently are found the white and red pines and white ash in the

This stand of sugar maple, beech and eastern hemlock in Pennsylvania is 120 years old.—*Photo courtesy U.S. Forest Service.*

North (see picture of southern New Hampshire forest), and the ironwood and buckeye in the South.

Lesser trees or tree canopies found under these large trees are the flowering dogwood, pigeonberry, hornbeam and redbud, while still lower down are such bushes or bushlike trees as the chokecherry and rhododendrons.

Where forests are young, the hemlock cannot grow because there is too much light for its seeds to start, but, sooner or later, other trees make it dark enough for the baby hemlocks to begin. If the other trees could understand, they would know that this beginning is the sign of their end, for the hemlocks keep growing up and up until their tops and finally their upper branches rise above other trees. Here the extraordinary hemlock needles, dark green above and with two light lines below, begin to take effect, for they appear on each twig in one flat, close-packed plane, and the many twigs overlap each other until sunlight can no longer penetrate them. When enough shade is thrown, the trees beneath begin to wither and die, and you can often see this beginning to happen wherever

Eastern Hemlock

Birch, beech, maple, hemlock, red and white pine forest of southern New Hampshire.—*Photo courtesy American Museum of Natural History.*

Eastern Hemlock

Beech

hemlocks begin to reach their height. Even the tallest maples, oaks, and birches can no longer compete. However, there are two trees that can stand up to the hemlock and fight back. One is the mighty white pine, and the other is the beech. Since the white pine has been cut down so much, it is the American beech, with its beautifully smooth gray bark, and its base spreading out to meet the roots in symmetrical ridges, that we are most likely to find associated with the hemlock in this forest, which, when fully grown, is a beech-hemlock climax forest that may last for ages if man leaves it alone.

In the beech-hemlock forest the two trees create a mood and a kind of tree symphony that is strange and delightful. When the wind is medium in strength, it plays through the hemlock tops with a kind of whistling sigh, as if the trees are saying, "Rest! Rest!" But, in the beech, the wind whispers and rustles with a sound almost like laughter, and it's entrancing to hear the sounds of both trees at once in the forest. All through the year, of course, the hemlock is a rhythm of dark brown and green, but the beech changes in mood from season to season, naked but grandly gray white in the winter and touched with shining light, then, as spring comes, beginning to flush with an almost ghostly green glow as the first leaves push out. The summer foliage is a translucent blue green that allows enough light to come through so that the beech-hemlock forest is spotted with light and dark according to which tree is above you. In fall the leaves of the beech turn a soft and golden yellow that clothe the tree in a more reverent light than the flamboyant colors of nearby maples. Then, when the leaves are first gone, the twigs are tinged with reddish brown, carrying among them the small, triangular-shaped dark nuts.

Because the hemlock is mainly a lover of the highlands, rocks, and streams with water leaping and laughing, it is in these places where beech and hemlock come together most often, both liking deep rich soil, but the beech also likes the rich bottomlands, and here it would stretch for miles if it were not for one

Mature stand of beech, maples, hemlocks, red and white pines, and ashes, grazed below by cattle.—*Photo courtesy Ontario Department of Natural Resources.*

creature, man, who has cut down the trees and plowed up the ground where the ancient forests stood. Only a few stands of these lowland beeches remain, but, where they do, you can sense what the pioneers once saw and knew when they walked or rode through those shady aisles of the great beech forests for hours.

Most of the forest that occupies what was once hemlock-beech climax forest today, however, is not the pure kind, but is a forest in transition, often kept that way by man or fire. In this forest the maples and the birches, and other trees, such as the basswoods, ashes, oaks, and hickories, often occupy a position as important as that of the beeches and hemlocks. Such a transitional forest reflects the characteristics of the typical deciduous forest, which will be discussed more fully in Chapter 8.

Eastern Hemlock

How to Tell Primitive from Advanced Trees

It seems wisest at this time, while we are talking about the mixture between the coniferous and deciduous forests as a whole, to consider those signs displayed by many eastern trees that show their place in evolution and their relations to the soil, to the weather or climate, and to each other.

The coniferous trees, scientists tell us, are among the most primitive of all trees and have been here on earth far longer than have the deciduous trees. What are the signs they give to show this? First, they bear their seeds naked in open cones instead of in closed receptacles, such as the fruits, nuts, and berries of the deciduous trees, which protect the seeds from outside influences. Second, with the exception of the tamarack in the North and the bald cypress in the South, they keep their needles on through the cold weather, unlike the deciduous trees which lose their leaves. These needles are able to continue on most coniferous trees in winter because of their heavy protection of a woodlike structure and a resinous covering, which is waterproof and an insulator. Another primitive feature of the coniferous trees—repeated, however, among some of the more primitive deciduous trees—is the distribution of their pollen for fertilization by the wind. Great clouds of this golden pollen are let loose in these forests in the springtime, appearing often like yellow rain.

Beech

The deciduous trees have evolved far beyond the primitive nature of the coniferous trees, as can be shown by a study of two tree characteristics: the kinds of flowers and the times of flowering. The kind, shape, and number of the petals, stamens, and pistils in the flowers tell us how far advanced a tree is in the scale of evolution. The old-fashioned flowers, the kind that lived on earth nearly as long ago as the dinosaurs, have numerous petals, stamens, and pistils. Typical of this kind of flower is the magnolia (see photo of flower of closely related tulip tree at the end of the section New Lumbering Ways That Save the Woods in Chapter 5). Like the willow, a less primitive tree, but with a great number of stamens also, the magnolia lets loose a cloud of yellow pollen that is carried broadcast by the wind, but some of it reaches the trees which need to be fertilized, very much as is done among the conifers. But more advanced flowers use insects to carry their pollen more specifically where it is needed instead of just anywhere with a hope that a few will reach their target. Such flowering trees have flowers with only a few petals, specialized in color and shape to attract bees and other insects to the few stamens and often only one pistil.

Sweetbay Magnolia

The time of flowering is also a sign which reveals how far advanced a tree

Pussy Willow

American Basswood

is, evolutionarily speaking. Primitive trees flower much earlier in the springtime because they depend on wind pollination, which is not dependent on the weather, but the more advanced flowers must wait for the insects to do the pollinating for them later, and so these trees come into flower later in spring.

Very early eastern trees coming into flowering in the springtime (in the order of their flowering) are: pussy willow, silver maple, red maple, elm, sugar maple, poplar, birch, oak, sweet gum, walnut, and hickory. They all produce what are called "short day flowers," which are pollinated mainly by the wind.

Some "long day flowers" and trees, whose flowers are pollinated by bees and other insects, are (in order of their flowering in spring): basswood, cherry, crab apple, locust, and hawthorns. Exact times of flowering vary of course according to latitude and altitude of each plant, with the trees in the North much later than those in the South.

Slow-growing vs. Fast-growing Trees

We have already noted that some trees have seedlings or young trees that grow best in the shade. Other trees start easily in sunlight as seedlings, but are killed by too much shade. The former are generally slow-growing large trees that become the dominant or climax trees of a forest, while the others are mainly fast-growing trees, adaptive to difficult situations of soil and slope, etc., but not generally having either very good lumber or staying power in the thick forests. The former are the trees man likes best for the lumber he needs for building, but his own use of these trees for building things being faster than they can reproduce themselves has actually encouraged the rapid spread of the less attractive lumber trees over wide areas. Many of these trees are what we call inventive or advanced evolutionary types, developing so many new varieties that scientists have a hard time keeping up with them. The hawthorns are an example, small trees so difficult to distinguish that even experts wring their hands over them, but yet so successful in our man-upset continent that they are spreading into all kinds of waste places and disturbed areas. The heath family, including the rhododendrons, mountain laurel, sourwood, and farkleberry, form a similar group of new-type trees, immensely successful on the edges of and even invading the forests and former areas that once supported much larger trees exclusively. Look for these kinds of new trees, not as just trees, a part of a forest mass, but as each having special characteristics that make them live and act in definite ways in our forests and woods.

Hawthorn

Rosebay
Rhododendron

SOUTHERN AND SOUTHEASTERN
PINE AND OAK-PINE WOODS

The main southern-type forests, outside of the mountains, are the pine or pine-oak woods, extending from the pine barrens of New Jersey to Texas, and including the oaks and pines in various combinations with the tulip tree and other trees in the piedmonts or uplands, and the pine savannas of the lower country in the Southeast and South through both the Atlantic and Gulf coastal plains. Most of these woods are not true climax forests, but successional, fire-influenced forests, largely caused by man cutting or burning out the large oaks and hickories that were once dominant over wide areas. It is interesting to note that while pines like the loblolly, shortleaf, and longleaf are secondary succes-

Forest on rim of Linville Gorge Wild Area, Pisgah National Forest, North Carolina, with pines, beeches, hemlocks, and rhododendrons.—*Photo courtesy U.S. Department of Agriculture.*

Virginia Pine

sional trees before the establishment of the climax forests, such trees as the scrub oak and scrub or Virginia pine take over from these larger pines and from the larger oaks when fires destroy the soil so much that the larger trees can no longer grow. They eventually rebuild the soil to the point where the other forest trees can move in.

The oak-pine forests and barrens of the area from southeastern New Jersey to Texas would be oak-hickory in climax, but fire and cutting has about eliminated the hickories, and the oak is found mainly where woods are old, in the case of the large oaks, or in newly burned or otherwise disturbed areas where the scrub oak takes over along with the pitch pine and the scrub pine. Some mixed oak-pine-tulip tree woods are found, as shown in the photograph taken in Chat-

Virgin loblolly pines mixed with oaks and other hardwoods in Chattahoochee National Forest, Georgia.—*Photo courtesy U.S. Forest Service.*

A good stand of pines, probably pitch, Virginia and/or shortleaf pines, in Maryland.—*Photo courtesy Library of Congress.*

Loblolly Pine

Pitch Pine

Shortleaf Pine

tahoochee National Forest, where loblolly pines are mixed with oaks. There are also some straight pine forests like the one in Maryland shown in the accompanying photograph. The loblolly and other southern pines shown in both pictures are typical of the successional generation of pines that take over so much of these forests that have been again and again burnt out and cut down.

Perhaps the best way to have a picture of the area is to discuss briefly some of the trees that now dominate it. In the north from Cape Cod to New Jersey and then south in the interior of foothill Virginia, pitch pine is the pine of the pine barrens, those dark wildernesses of mainly sandy soils where fire is always a terrible hazard and where the sweet pitchy odor of the pines comes on the wind. The three twisted, rigid, and very dark green needles in each bundle are distinctive, as are the small brown cones, later turning black and dead-looking. So often have these pines been burned and cut that they are now mostly pygmies of their former selves and they are much invaded by scrub oaks.

To the south the 2- or 3-needled shortleaf pines take over on the richer lands of the foothills, with 2-needled scrub or Virginia pines holding down the wastelands and the recently burnt-over areas. With them and the pitch pine in most of this area is found the distinctive chestnut oak, with its acorns enclosed one-third of the way up in a peculiar-looking cup of fused scales. It is a hillside and dry-land tree. In richer bottoms the chinquapin oak flashes its bicolored leaves, yellow-green above and silvery below. Another oak of the uplands and dry, infertile soils is the southern red oak, distinctive for its very small, half-inch-long acorns. The black oak has similar leaves, but a slightly larger acorn, half-covered with a much-fringed cup. The lustrous bright green leaves of the scarlet oak, an important inhabitant of upland light sandy soils, are most noted for the far more brilliant scarlet they turn into in fall, filling the forest with flame. The shagbark and butternut hickory are two other trees that would be much more common save for cutting by man. And, to the south, the tulip trees are frequent companions of the oaks and pines (commonly the loblolly pines) in moister areas.

Over much of the central and southern part of the oak-pine area there brood the ghosts of the great battles of the Civil War, and there are trees alive yet that hold within their trunks bullets and shell fragments fired in that war. The sign

Longleaf pine grove near Guntersville Dam, Alabama.—*Photo courtesy Tennessee Valley Authority.*

of poorness brought on the land by the destruction of that war and continued by man's destruction of the trees and soil since is the coming into poor soil areas of the blackjack or scrub oak, which is hardly more than a shrub. Its one saving grace is that eventually it may help make that soil good enough to hold larger and more important trees.

Though because of the almost yearly burning of the undercover grass, pine forests and savannas are dominant over much of the yellow soil of the coastal plains of both the Atlantic and Gulf of Mexico, they mix with deciduous trees in areas where there is more moisture. In drier or more frequently burned and cut areas, they appear mainly as strictly pine forests, or as pine savannas (see accompanying photos). In the savannas the very inflammable wire grass is often the dominant or only undercover. The fires started in this grass each summer tend to destroy shrubs and very young trees, leaving the pines standing as masters of the region. Wherever man protects the forest from this yearly fire, the hardwood deciduous shrubs and trees begin to grow, and the soil becomes richer. Trees that come back include the oaks (particularly the turkey, laurel, and live oaks), tulip tree, magnolias, sweet gum, basswood, hickories, and black cherry.

Blackjack Oak

Turkey Oak

This longleaf pine savannah in Florida is 80 years old.—*Photo courtesy U.S. Forest Service.*

Longleaf Pine

Shortleaf Pine

Slash Pine

Virginia Pine

The burned-out, cut-over, or worked-out fields and woods of the South, particularly on the coastal plains of the Atlantic and Gulf, have been taken over largely by the pine savanna, where the rosemary scent of the loblolly pine's incense comes on the breeze. The five most important pines of the area can be quickly told apart by the following brief chart:

Dominant Pines of the Atlantic and Gulf Coastal Plains

Name of pine	Leaf	Bark	Cone	Range
Longleaf	8-18 in., 3 needles in bundle, bright green.	Orange brown with papery scales.	6-10 in. long, reddish brown; scale with small prickle.	Whole area.
Loblolly	6-9 in., 3 needles, pale green.	Reddish brown, scalelike plates.	3-6 in. long, reddish brown; scale with sharp tooth.	Most of area.
Shortleaf	3-5 in., 2-3 needles, dark bluish green.	Reddish orange with irregular grooves.	1 1/2-2 1/2 in. long, reddish brown, lightly speckled.	Whole area.
Slash pine	8-12 in., 2-3 or more needles in bundle; shiny, dark green.	Orange, with large, loose plates.	3-6 in. long, lustrous brown.	S.E. part of area.
Virginia or scrub pine	1 1/2-3 in., 2 needles in bundle, gray green.	Dark brown red or orange brown; plate-like scales.	1 1/2-2 1/2 in. long, reddish brown, inner lip of scale with purple stripe.	N.E. part of area and south to South Carolina.

Probably the most important timber tree of these is the longleaf pine, while the Virginia or scrub pine is the least important timberwise, but the latter is very important as an aggressive nurse tree that can grow in and rebuild very rocky or sterile soil that the three main pines cannot handle. At first the scrub pine forms large thickets, taking over from broom sedge, its most common forerunner, and then becoming so dense that nothing can get a foothold in the thicket except the Japanese honeysuckle and catbriers. Perhaps twenty-five years later dogwood and redbud begin to grow in the stand, enriching the soil, and opening it out eventually so that larger pines and the seedlings of other large trees can get a foothold in the now richer soil and then finally take over. Watching for these signs, we can tell what stages of succession these areas are in.

The slash pine, though growing bigger than the Virginia or scrub pine, often serves the same aggressive purpose further south of taking over abandoned and sterile land, though more in the bottom and damp places. All of these pines except the scrub pine have long clear trunks when they are grown, which is what the lumberman wants, but the longleaf, loblolly, and shortleaf pines are the ones most grown on pine plantations. The longleaf pine has one noteworthy peculiarity, "the grass state." In this state, a whole group of these young pines may appear above ground only as a dense cluster of what look like small branches covered with needles. This state may persist four or more years. Actually, each tree is growing at a prodigious rate, but all underground! A great central tap root and myriads of side roots are being formed during this time from which the tree will begin, when the time is right, to spring up to its major height.

A summer spent in one of these pine savannas will bring back lasting memories of the high whisper of the wind playing with the needles far above you, the warm aroma of pine resin baking in the sun, and the hot scent of the yellow or red earth rising through the shallow leaf mold. Sometimes such shrubs and small trees as flowering dogwood, mountain laurel, willow oak, live oak, southern bayberry, and loblolly bay—their flowers blooming white, rose, pink, and yellow—spring up too, under the pines.

Longleaf Pine

CONIFEROUS FORESTS OF THE WEST

If our western coniferous forests can be thought of as great dark seas, then the crests of some of the waves of those seas, foaming in white and gold, are the beautiful quaking aspens that act as nursemaids to the young conifers. These forests have within them the greatest and most magnificent of all trees in the world, giants often reaching over two hundred and fifty and some over three hundred feet in height, far outreaching the trees of the East. Other trees of the high mountains, the bristlecone pines, are not giants, yet so old that their beginnings, in some individuals, extend back more than two thousand years before the time of Christ; some perhaps are as ancient as the pyramids of Egypt and thus the oldest of all living things. If they were sentient beings, with what pity they could look down upon us, insectlike creatures whose lives are but as a day in their lives! None of these trees can talk, but signs wonderful and strange we can read among them, as you shall see.

Trembling Aspen

SUBALPINE FORESTS

Few more dramatic, stern, and vigorous places can be found on the face of the globe than timberline and the trees just below it in the Rockies, Cascades, and Sierras of the West. Here the trees reach peakward with their last little waves of green, ending in tiny foot-high trees, lost among the rocks, or trees so wrenched and squashed by wind and snow that they are flattened out on the ground. Here many a tree, such as the Engelmann spruce of the Rockies, tries vainly to reach its tip above the deep snows of winter in some high glade, only to have that tip knocked off year after year, not so much by the strike of the high winds, but by their searing dryness in those cold, dry winters, the opposite and yet the same as the hot dryness of the khamsin, the wind that sears all life on the Sahara Desert. Here also, a tree is frequently driven by the wind to grow its branches out almost entirely on one side, and the branches grow farther and farther out (see What Wind Does in Chapter 2), while the top stays always the same, no higher than the snow is deep. Watch for this among the high peaks,

Engelmann Spruce

Limber Pine

Engelmann Spruce

Alpine Fir

and see also where such trees, only a few feet high, may form a continuous mat across the ground, making a forest whose tops you can walk on!

From these timberline trees you can look out over the ranges and see on distant high ridges the same high-altitude trees repeated, an indication that the wind has reached across the miles with the pollen, or the seeds may be carried by high-altitude birds, like the Clark's nutcracker, from peak to peak.

If we move in a great arc from northern New Mexico, north through the Rockies, then across to the Cascades and down through the Sierras, always following up near the tops of the peaks, we can see how the timberline trees and the subalpine forest, whose highest rim they are, change and vary somewhat from region to region, though maintaining some of the same trees and characteristics in all regions. In effect, this is the great northern spruce-fir forest, riding down the tops of the mountains out of Canada, first around 4,000 feet in the Canadian Rockies and ending up at about 10,000 feet or so in the southern Rockies.

Southern and Central Rockies Subalpine Forest

Trees found mainly at timberline here are the bristlecone pine, with five 1/2-1 1/2-inch-long needles and shallow-furrowed reddish brown bark, and the limber pine, also with five needles, but these 1 1/2 to 3 inches long, and with deeply furrowed dark brown bark. The important subalpine trees that stretch some of their members up to timberline are the Engelmann spruce, with its thin, dark blue, very pliant needles; the alpine fir, with its very stiff, up-curving, deep bluish green needles, and the lodgepole pine, with 2-3 needles in a bundle, found somewhat lower, but often a subalpine tree. It is interesting to watch the march of the spruce and fir to timberline. Both have very thin spirelike forms in dense forests, but the alpine fir keeps this beautiful form even when standing alone, and marches right up to the highest places on the ranges in ranks like straight-standing soldiers, refusing to bow to the heaviest snow, though the first at timberline are limited by cold and wind to a height of about a foot! The Engelmann spruce, on the other hand, is twisted by both wind and snow into various grotesque forms, often flattening out in the direction of wind blow. Strangely

Timberline trees at head of Hondo River in New Mexico Rockies, including Engelmann spruce, alpine fir, limber pine, etc.—*Photo courtesy U.S. Forest Service.*

Subalpine forest of Engelmann spruce and alpine fir in Colorado Rockies.—*Photo courtesy U.S. Department of Agriculture.*

enough, it is the fir that has the weaker wood of the two, not good enough for most building lumber, but the fir seems to have some other kind of toughness that enables it to face the winds. And always the inevitable quaking aspens creep in among the spruce and fir or seize newly burned ground for their own until new firs and spruces outgrow and outshade them.

Northern Rockies Subalpine Forest

Limber pine, of the lightly grooved reddish brown bark, is found here at timberline, but is always a loner, a tree that loves isolated places among the rocks where few other trees like to be. The whitebark pine, gleaming with white bark, the subalpine fir, the mountain hemlock, and the lodgepole pine are the common trees of this area.

Whitebark Pine

Cascade and British Columbian Subalpine Forest

There are no trees in this area found solely in the timberline, but the whitebark pine, the alpine fir, the mountain hemlock, and the lodgepole pine are the common trees of this region.

Mountain Hemlock

Sierra Nevadan Subalpine Forest

The foxtail pine, with its reddish brown bark and bright bluish green needles in bundles of five, is a unique timberline tree of the high Sierras, being another loner, like the limber pine, on high, isolated rocky places, where it is twisted and warped by the winds. Coming up to join it and usually much outnumbering it, are the whitebark pines, and some mountain hemlocks, with their thick, short, blue gray to pale green needles and their bowing tops. A bit lower, lodgepole pines and quaking aspens make their appearance, particularly in burned-over or lumber-cut areas.

Foxtail Pine

Subalpine Grasses and Flowers

It is interesting to drive up through these forests in the summer on the high mountain passes, such as Tioga Pass in California, Beartooth Pass in Wyoming, Logan Pass in Montana, or Fall River Pass in Colorado, and find where the last snowdrifts are melting to break loose the alpine flowers and grass from the snow-wetted soil. Here alpine timothy grass lifts its thickly floreted panicles, bear grass (not a true grass at all) flashes its white or cream flowers in an immense pyramid at the top of the stalk, and green false hellebore raises its immense, coarse-grained, corrugated leaves. You may also find the creamy-white flowers of the death camas, lifting up in a loose raceme from its thick-coated poisonous bulb. Then the numerous deep sulphur-yellow flowers of the sulphur flower nod in the breeze, along with the large and showy bluish-tinged flowers of the western windflower. Most of these and many other flowers in this area find identical species or close relatives in other high mountains ringing the entire Northern Hemisphere. This tells us that, at the time of the great glaciers, these flowers may have extended for far greater distances.

Adaptive Trees of the Subalpine

Some of the adaptations of individual trees to the great cold, deep snow, and high winds of the subalpine forests are extremely interesting. Remember that often these mountains are hit by winds traveling at such tremendous speeds that they carry with them sand and dirt particles from far-off deserts that act like rough sandpaper on the sides of the trees. Remember also that the temperature in winter often plunges to fifty degrees below zero or lower, and that the snow in some years may last all summer long and until the next snow falls. In fact, one of the peculiarities of some subalpine trees caught in these deep, long-lasting snows is that they may have two or more years in which they have no growing season at all, but simply stay dormant until enough sunlight finally comes one summer to break them loose from their prison. In such cases the trees will show no growth rings, which means a tree with forty rings in its trunk may actually be fifty years or more old!

Limber Pine

The limber pine is a tree which adapts to its place among the most wind-blown rocks and cliffs by having such easily bendable branches that we can actually tie the twigs into knots without breaking them! This allows the tree not only to bend before the wind, but to quickly drop off a heavy load of wet snow whenever it gets too thick on the branches. The bristlecone and foxtail pines are other good examples of what are called "wind timber" because of the way they are molded by the wind. In fact, the bristlecone pines, as shown in the accompanying picture, may actually be so scoured by the sandpaperlike quality of the sand-filled gales that hit these mountaintops that the bark is rasped completely off the windward side, and the trees are able to keep the cambium in activity only on the leeward side. Sometimes the branches and even the trunks may be twisted like corkscrews by the unimaginable force. Despite such a difficult life, it is not uncommon to find a tree no higher than a man with the hoary age of 900 or more years! As already pointed out, some of the grand old monarchs of bristlecone pine in the White Mountains of western Nevada and eastern California have been found to be the oldest living things, with ages close to 5,000 years! What tenacity of life in such extreme conditions of cold and wind!

Foxtail Pine

The Lodgepole Pine Forests

The lodgepole pine is mainly a tree of the lower part of the subalpine forest and just below. It is a tree that strangely looks either like a noble specimen of

Bristlecone pines on Mt. Evans in the Colorado Rockies.—*Photo by Alfred M. Bailey.*

pine, standing straight and fine-limbed, when found alone, or a scraggly pole with half or more of its trunk still clinging uselessly to a clutter of dead limbs, when found in its usual dense stands. It almost seems as if the tree deliberately tries to be a firebrand, and there is a queerly good reason for this, as the seeds in the usually closed cones of this tree are best let loose by the heat of a raging fire. It is a tree that creeps into meadows, filled-in surfaces of old beaver ponds, and burnt or cut-over areas, very much like the quaking aspen, but not nearly as beautiful. It spreads because it is able to grow in open sunlit spaces and poor soil that the nobler firs and spruces do not like. You usually can tell it is a fire-advent tree by the fact that it so often grows in stands of uniform height, showing the seeds were sowed all in the same year by the coming of the fire. Ordinarily we would be glad to have a tree like this come in and take over a burnt area to rebuild the soil, but the lodgepole pine has the drawback of being so inflammable that young fir and spruce trees often don't get a chance to grow up before a fire comes and burns them out. Thus a lodgepole pine forest may renew itself through fire but stop other trees from taking over. Since the lodgepole forest is also exceedingly difficult to walk through because of all the dead branches, we would much prefer the quaking aspen as the nurse tree for new firs and spruces.

Lodgepole pine forest in Targhee National Forest, Idaho.—*Photo courtesy U.S. Forest Service.*

MIDDLE-ALTITUDE ROCKY MOUNTAIN FORESTS

Rocky Mt. Juniper

One-Leaved Pinyon
Pine

In the middle altitudes of the Rockies are found their great forests and also the beautiful mountain parks, as they are called, gleaming stretches of meadowland between the forests where deer and elk love to graze as well as cattle. Amid the massive motifs of the peaks, eternally tipped with snow, the vast green flanks of the Rockies inspire us with thoughts of America the Beautiful and how we must work to make all our land a similar Garden of Eden.

As you go up into the Rockies from the foothills, you see the signs of coming events every two or three thousand feet you climb, either afoot or by car. Look to the north- and south-facing slopes of a canyon to get your key. In the foothills you have left the grasslands behind on the plain below, but you have entered into the region of the pinyon-juniper forest, which not only includes the juniper and pinyon pine (see Intermountain Pinyon-Juniper Woodlands later in this chapter), but also various bushes, such as the mountain mahogany and the scrub oak. Gradually, as you travel higher, these plants move over to the south-facing slopes, and you begin to see on the north-facing slopes the ponderosa pines, forerunners of the ponderosa pine forest, which completely supplants the pinyons and junipers at a higher elevation.

Keep climbing and notice the first change when you see that the ponderosa pines have moved over to the south-facing slopes, while the dark bluish green ranks of the Douglas fir begin to appear on the north-facing slopes (illustrated perfectly in the photograph). Soon, as you climb still higher, the Douglas fir and the Colorado blue spruce become the dominant trees everywhere about you, but another thousand feet higher and you find the Douglas fir has moved to the south-facing slopes while the Engelmann spruce is appearing on the north-facing slopes with its thin spirelike shape. As you get up into the main spruce forest of the subalpine zone, it changes gradually into the spruce-fir forest already described, as the alpine fir joins the spruce, and the two kinds of spirelike trees sweep up the mountainside to the timberline. Something of this relation of trees to shade and sun on north- and south-facing slopes has already been described under What Shade Does to Plants in Chapter 1.

Looking up Red River Canyon to Wheeler Peak in New Mexico. Ponderosa pine forest is on south-facing slope, and Douglas fir-Colorado blue spruce forest (with the darker trees) is on north-facing slope.—*Photo courtesy U.S. Forest Service.*

Ponderosa Pine Forests

The ponderosa pines are noted for both the high clear singing of the wind in their needles and their open stands through which the light of the sun comes easily. Their forest in the Rockies is considerably more open than where it joins with other trees and shrubs on the western slopes of the Sierras. Though not often as tall as the Douglas fir, it is a more massive tree and is told from most other pines by its yellow green needles in bundles of three, and its bark, which in grown trees is a bright cinnamon red and broken into large plates, with a peculiar series of irregularly lobed sections that resemble a picture puzzle. In summer the scent of the air among these pines spells wilderness and purity, and, to walk among them is to walk among benign giants with little of the feeling of darkness you often meet with in the higher forests of the Rockies.

Ponderosa Pine

Though the ponderosa pine seems to like living in large groves of its own kind alone, it is often penetrated by white fir in the south and central Rockies, and by western red cedar, western larch and western white pine in the northern Rockies. Though grasses of various kinds, especially blue grass or grama, are mainly found under these well-spaced trees, shrubs like mountain mahogany, scrub oaks, and western sagebrush often penetrate these forests, especially where fire or man has cleared away parts of them. The grass under these trees is so much appreciated by cattle and sheep that ranchers move their herds into the mountains in the hot summers, and we may begin to see signs in late summer of overgrazing, such as short-cropped grass and the destruction of young seedling trees (see The Results of Overgrazing in Chapter 5). Erosion is often started, and a whole forest can be ruined in time. The U. S. Forest Service has been putting the brakes on this practice, but the sheepmen and cattlemen pressure for more, not less grazing privileges, not realizing that the destruction of the trees and grass can hurt them too in time.

Douglas Fir

White Fir

Douglas Fir and Blue Spruce Forests

The Douglas fir is really not a fir at all, but it has no common name that fits it, except possibly the recently suggested one of "Douglastree." However, it is

Mature ponderosa pine forest near Lincoln, Montana.—*Photo courtesy U.S. Department of Agriculture.*

the most extensive and valuable of all our forest trees and one of the greatest in size and height. It is also very easy to identify, for all you have to do is look at one of the small cones and see that each ribbon-shaped bract between the scales has a three-forked tongue. Another distinctive feature is the many long slender twigs, each spiraled with numerous needles, that hang straight down from the branches like so many little tails. When a storm hits the forest, these "tails" begin to stream before it like the wild hair of witches, while a seething roaring sounds above you, and the mass of trees appears to writhe like some great loose-furred monster.

The dark bluish green of the Douglas fir, and its companion in the southern and central Rockies, the Colorado blue spruce of the canyon bottoms, makes a sharp color break from the yellow green of the ponderosa pine forest below (see photo of Red River Canyon under Middle-Altitude Rocky Mountain Forests above). But the same Douglas fir-blue spruce forest seems to merge imperceptibly colorwise into the equally dark bluish green Engelmann spruce and alpine fir forests of the subalpine zone above. However, look closely and you will soon see that these higher-altitude trees are more thin and spirelike than the bulkier Douglas firs and blue spruces below. In the southern and central Rockies the white fir comes up into the Douglas fir forest from its main ground beside the ponderosa pines, but, in the northern Rockies, the grand fir and the hemlocks (western and mountain) take its place.

Throughout the whole Rocky Mountains fire and the cutting by man into the grand old Douglas fir forests open the way for either the quaking aspen or the fire-seeding lodgepole pine to take over the new sunlit spaces. The quick-growing, quick-dying aspens, with their twinkling leaves letting in the sunlight, but not too much, make the best nurse trees for the young Douglas firs, but the pines can both make too much shade and be dangerous firetraps (see The Lodgepole Pine Forests earlier in this chapter).

In the northern Rockies the western and mountain hemlocks are shade-loving trees that actually grow better in the dark fir forests and may eventually rise to drown out with shade the young firs and take their place. The large lumber companies have learned that the answer to this is block and strip cutting of the fir forests (see New Lumbering Ways That Save the Woods in Chapter 5),

Trembling Aspen

SEED

Mountain Hemlock

Colorado blue spruce and Nuttall's willow in Colorado Rockies.—*Photo by Alfred M. Bailey.*

Western larch are the lighter-colored trees in forest of Valley County, Idaho, that also includes ponderosa pine, white fir, Douglas fir, and lodgepole pine.—*Photo courtesy U.S. Forest Service.*

allowing the seedlings to be nursed into production by aspens in the cut-over areas.

Western Larch, White Pine, and Red Cedar Forest

This forest is found mainly in northern Idaho, northwestern Montana, and southeastern British Columbia. At first glance one might think he is among ponderosa pines when he sees the western larch trees, as they have the same cinnamon red, plated bark, and the same color in their yellow green needles. However, a closer look soon shows that the needles are in bundles of fifteen to thirty, far more than any pine ever has, and also far shorter, only 1 to 1 1/4 inches long. The light brown cones are also much tinier than pinecones, or only 1 to 1 1/2 inches long.

Western Larch

The western white pine can be told by its dark violet-gray to reddish bark, its five pale blue-green needles in a bundle, and its short, drooping branches. The western red cedar is almost immediately recognized by its fernlike sprays of branchlets covered with dark green overlapping and spicy-smelling scales, and its peculiar budlike cones. The grand fir and also the western hemlock are fine members of this forest.

Western White Pine

This is a dark and gloomy forest in its virgin stands, the high branches interlocking like a tight umbrella, and opening up mainly when fire or cutting has happened, with quaking aspen or lodgepole pine temporarily taking over. It is a forest that has the dubious honor of producing the most terrible fire in United States history. In the very dry, hot summer of 1910, careless cutting and burning of trash by lumbermen combined with a far understaffed U.S. Forestry Service crew resulted in a calamity on August 20, when over 3,000 small fires were already turning the air blue over most of Idaho. Suddenly that day these small flames exploded into one vast blazing inferno that destroyed homes, farms, whole towns, railroad trains, and lumberyards. Never again would the people of Idaho laugh at and discourage the forest rangers and their efforts to save the forests, as they did in the "good old days" before that terrible fire. Even today some of the dead black stumps of that great fire loom out of the new green in many parts of the mountains. The forest came back, but man had better not be that careless again!

INTERMOUNTAIN PINYON-JUNIPER WOODLANDS

The cougar, or mountain lion, generally likes the region of the pinyon-juniper woodland because it is rocky and rough, with many caves and large rock crevices to hide in, and very poor land for either ranches or farms, so that not many human beings are around to bother him. Winds blow hard through the cedar breaks, as these woods are called by some local people, and the winds roar over the rimrock at the trees on the plateaus and mesas with a great shouting. The junipers, however, are more twisted and rasped by this wind power, as they choose to grow on the more exposed ridges and cliffs, while the pines make more of an attempt to stand upright by growing in more sheltered swales or flats.

One-Leaved Pinyon
Pine

Pinyon pine nuts are food to many animals and are still gathered by Indians and by those whites who have learned to appreciate their delicious nut flavor and their fine qualities of nourishment. The common pinyon pines are the one-leaved pinyon and the two-leaved pinyon, the first with dull brown to gray bark, the latter with reddish brown bark. The junipers are rather hard to tell apart. Most have bluish black, strongly aromatic berries, except for the alligator juniper, which has dull reddish brown berries and strange bark, looking like alligator skin; the Utah juniper, which also has reddish brown berries, and the California junipers, which have green berries. Like the pinyon nuts, these berries are eaten by many animals and birds, principally the pinyon jay, and, in the old days, the Indians sometimes ground the berries up and mixed them with other wild foods. The Indians also used juniper bark for diapers, bedding, and starting fires. It is obviously very soft!

Mountain Mahogany

Some other common plants found among the pinyon-juniper woods are the Apache plume, common sagebrush, antelope bush, mountain mahogany, and various sharp-spined yuccas.

In these woods you can usually tell the direction from which the prevailing winds come by the way the windward sides of these trees, particularly the junipers, often have the bark completely rasped off by flying sand. Frequently several branches are killed by the wind, and these are knocked or cut off by

Pinyon-juniper woodland in Southwest. Two-leaved pinyon pine is shown in insert.—
Photo courtesy C. J. Grimes, National Park Service. Insert photo by Alfred M. Bailey.

ranchers in the region for firewood. The live wood is almost impossible to cut through with an axe, as I have found out on several occasions in Colorado, but the dead wood is brittle and burns with a good flame. The toughness of some old junipers is remarkable. They stand, twisted and gnarled, on rocky crags where they have been scoured by wind for half a thousand years or more and look as though they can go on forever!

Western Juniper

MIDDLE SIERRA AND SOUTHERN CASCADE FORESTS

The Sierras and the southern Cascades are in the rain shadow of the Pacific Ocean, from which rain sweeps inland over the lower coast ranges. Rain hits the lower flanks, and then snow usually comes in great quantities to the middle altitudes of the mountains in winter, creating the snow forest with snow often over twenty feet deep. The east sides of these mountain ranges are very steep, entirely different from the western slopes, much dryer, with wider-spread trees and more closely related to the forests of the Rockies in composition and quality. The ponderosa pine is replaced on the east slope by the closely related Jeffrey pine, which has a vanillalike fragrance. From about the middle of Oregon north the Cascades become Douglas fir-oriented in their main forests, and the ponderosa pines rather paradoxically pass over to the east side of the ranges, where the climate is dryer. Evidently the ponderosa cannot stand the increased rain and snow of the northern Cascades, a damp territory indeed!

Jeffrey Pine

Ponderosa Pine Forests and the Big Trees

As soon as you drive through the blue oaks and digger pines of the Sierra foothills, you climb into sweet-smelling forests of the ponderosa and sugar pines.

Digger Pine

Virgin ponderosa pine stand in Lassen National Forest, California.—*Photo courtesy U.S. Forest Service.*

Giant sequoias in Sierras.—*Photo courtesy U.S. Forest Service.*

The former tree has yellowish green needles, three to the bundle, while the latter has dark bluish green needles, five to the bundle. The ponderosa has short, thick cones, while the sugar pine has very long, slender cones, and is also told by the sweet smell and taste of its sap. The incense cedar and the white fir are other large trees common in this area. Three lesser but very common trees are the black oak; the Pacific dogwood, with great white blooms that flower in May, and the beautifully climbing vine maple.

Giant Sequoia

This is a forest of giants rising above giants—the ponderosa pine, with massive trunks that reach topmost branches as high as 220 feet, the sugar pine, greatest of all living pine trees, reaching as high as 245 feet, but both far overtopped by the king tree, the giant sequoia, shoving a top or two above 270 feet. It is impossible to enter these great forests without being awed by their vastness and the feeling of almost infinite growth. The giant sequoia is not as tall as the highest coast redwoods, but it is far greater in bulk, some trees weighing over 600 tons and with over 120,000 board feet of lumber, enough to build several houses!

The groves of these vast trees (the sequoias) are isolated from each other in the middle and southern Sierras, at the beginning of the snow forest, between 8,000 and 6,000 feet altitude. This is a sign of a time when they spread over far wider areas millions of years in the past. Look at a trunk twenty to twenty-five feet thick; gaze skyward and see a branch as much as ten stories or more above you, seven feet thick at its base, and itself as big as many a tree called big in other lands. How puny is man, how petty his feverish digging for the will-o'-the-wisp of gold in these same hills, when compared to such a giant and its three thousand years or more of life! Pause, think, and be humble.

The Red Fir Forest

Red Fir

Higher than the big trees is the true snow forest of the red firs, their soldier-like massed ranks of beautifully symmetrical cone-shaped trees telling us of deep, rich soil so gently, thoroughly, sustainedly watered by twenty- to thirty-foot-deep drifts of melting snow that far into summer the dark soil beneath these fairylike trees is still strong with dampness. Only in the northern Cascades and in British Columbia is there found deeper snow in America. Here also the roots of the trees, the deep layers of leaf mold, and the dank shade protect the underground water so that all through the hot California summer the crystal streams of the mountains pour down the slopes to supply irrigation water to the thirsty farms so far below.

SEED

Foxtail Pine

Interesting to know is that the red fir is a parent welcomed by its young ones, for the young trees grow well in the dark shade under the large adults, a feature many other trees do not possess, for their seedlings must have light to grow. This wonderful cooperation between red fir generations is one explanation for the vast success of these forests and the complete dominance in the main snow forest of this one kind of tree. Perhaps there is a lesson here for human generations, if we could only find it. But the red firs are trees of the wide flats just before the final peaks, liking the shelter from the wind of the higher ridges, and massing together themselves to keep out the wind that screams through the passes. There are no adventurers in this forest, ready to brave the crags of the mountains, none ready to sacrifice their beauty for the gnarled misshapen figures of foxtail and whitebark pines that crouch indomitably on the windswept cliffs.

Whitebark Pine

Here is beauty among trees indeed, not dominance and might like that of

Virgin red fir forest with small firs showing their ability to grow in shade of big trees.—*Photo courtesy U.S. Forest Service.*

Red Fir

the big tree, but we can see a craving for perfection in the large purplish brown cones that stand erect on the red firs in fall, looking as if carved by a master artist and painted with transparent but gleaming crystal, as indeed they are when you examine them and find a coating of crystalline basalm, the same that is used in microscope mounts.

Under these firs grow few other trees, but some associated ones on the fringes are the white fir, western white pine, lodgepole pine, mountain hemlock, and Douglas fir.

PACIFIC COASTAL CONIFEROUS FORESTS

When the magnificent white pine forests of the East were exhausted by fire and ruthless lumbering, the Tyees, or lumber company tycoons, gave out a great sigh of relief when they learned about the vast forests of the Pacific Northwest, forests so titanic they foolishly dreamed they would be inexhaustible. But even these vast forests are showing signs of ending now, and the Tyees, wiser we hope, and probably sadder, are being forced into tree farming on a gigantic scale. May the wisdom of all of us grow before it is too late, and the finest forests in the world crumble and fade away before the ruthless onslaught of man.

The Redwood Forest

Redwood

Trees of mystery they have been called and trees of the mist they truly are, for it is the long, low clouds of summer fog, rolling landward all during the hot summer months of northwestern California and southwestern Oregon that keep the great redwood forests damp and dripping so they can continue to live until

Virgin redwood forest in Del Norte County, California, with sword ferns and huckleberry bushes, etc. underneath.—*Photo courtesy U.S. Department of Agriculture.*

the late fall rains come to give them their normal wetting. Walk through the eternal shade of these great forests, under trees that commonly reach above 300 feet into the sky and include the tallest trees on earth, one having been found with a height over 380 feet, and you know you walk in the Presence! At the feet of these masters of growth there may be absolute stillness, and perfect shade, with not a breeze blowing, but perhaps thirty stories above ground, if you listen closely, you can hear a slow, deep breathing, the breath of the wind blowing through a hundred great tops that lie up there in glaring sunlight. Look about you and you see one of the loveliest carpets ever put under trees. It is made up of the green velvet leaves of the three-leaved redwood sorrels, with great clumps of sword ferns on guard around their fringes, then here and there the pink, delicate flower of a redwood orchid, the white, foamlike flowers of ocean spray, or the great wide three-lobed leaflets of deer-foot, while every fallen log or buttress of a mighty trunk seems covered an inch or more deep with dark green moss. These are living things that delight in shade, a shade so deep that few other trees, except an occasional red alder near a stream or a gray-barked tanbark oak, finding some small opening where a bit of sunlight streams down, rise among those great trunks. A bush, however, also likes the shade, and some areas under the redwoods are covered with the bright green leaves and delicious red or black berries of the red or black huckleberry.

Redwood

Redwood Sorrel

Red Huckleberry

The huge buttresses that reach out from the trunks help support the mass of wood above and are needed, for the redwood's root system, though widespread, is shallow. Often we see signs of where fire has come and eaten into the heart of a tree, enough sometimes to make a room in which a hermit could, and, occasionally has, lived! But the bark of the redwood is fire-resistant, and it takes a pretty strong fire to do the damage we see in some of these trees.

On the trunks, or even on the massive limbs, there sometimes appear strange-looking bumps, as if the tree had developed boils. These are redwood burls, which may have been caused by disease, insect work, or some foreign object getting into the wood. Whatever the cause, the burls have much different wood from the main part of the trunk, very hard and often with intricate and beautiful designs when sawn into sections. Pieces of burls are sold in gift shops and can be taken home and put in shallow water. From them grow beautiful feathery redwood branches, as if you had brought the living tree into your home. Indeed, a redwood tree knocked down by saw and wedge is not truly dead, because, from the stump a ring of new young trees will spring up, not seed trees, but true parts of the fallen giant, continuing its life, something that may endure through a thousand centuries or more in deathless recreation of grandeur! Often, in cut-over redwood forests, you will find circles of young trees and can be fairly certain that they circle the place where once stood a grand monarch.

The Pacific Coastal Douglas Fir Forest

We have already met the Douglas fir forest in the Rocky Mountains earlier in this chapter, so, on the Pacific Coast, we can recognize it and the three little tongues in each bract of its cones, as old friends. But the Pacific Coast is a damper area with deeper soil, and here the Douglas fir grows higher (sometimes over 220 feet) and broader (often more than 17 feet in diameter). Everywhere it is the premier lumber tree of America, and is being farmed extensively by great lumber companies, like Weyerhauser and American Forest Products Corporation. In

Douglas Fir

the forests of the Pacific Coast the Douglas fir is surpassed in size only by the redwood and, to the redwood, it frequently acts as a nurse tree in areas where redwoods have been cut out. Beyond the fog area and in the cooler climate to northward where the redwood cannot grow, the Douglas fir is the premier tree over vast areas, though trimmed greatly by the lumberman and his saw.

In the Sierras the Douglas fir is just another tree, but, in northwestern California, the Oregon and Washington coasts, and far up into the northern Cascades and the mountains of British Columbia it often becomes the main climax tree. Only among the redwoods and in the deep rain forest of the Olympic Peninsula, where the Sitka spruce is king, does it take second place. Associated with it in all this wide and long region are the western white pine, in the Cascades and British Columbia, while the grand fir, the Sitka spruce, and the western red cedar are common with it in the lower country. Lesser trees, often found where the Douglas fir grows, are the California black oak, the western chokecherry, Pacific madrone, the vine maple and broad-leaf maple, the Pacific dogwood, the Oregon ash, and the California laurel (called the Oregon myrtle in Oregon).

Wander into a Douglas fir forest and, if you find young western hemlocks growing under it, you will know these are shade-loving trees that may eventually supplant the Douglas fir forest in that area in time if not cut out. This is because the Douglas fir seedlings do not like that deep shade and cannot grow there to compete with the hemlock youngsters, which will take over when the old Douglas firs die. The lumberjack knows this, which is why he block or strip cuts Douglas fir forests (see New Lumbering Ways That Save the Woods in Chapter 5) these days in order to give the fir seedlings a place under the sun where they can grow and produce new forests. Conversely, a western hemlock forest jealously keeps Douglas firs out and allows only its own shade-loving seedlings to grow.

The Closed-Cone Pine Forest

Here and there along the Pacific Coast are strange little forests of sometimes rare species of pine trees and cypresses, usually called the closed-cone pine forests, because some of the pines have cones that rarely open their scales.

California Black Oak

Madrone

Oregon Ash

Douglas fir timber in Willamette National Forest, Oregon, with thimbleberry and other shrubs below.—*Photo courtesy U.S. Forest Service.*

Beach and bishop pines on rocky coast of Mendocino County, California.—*Photo courtesy Redwood Empire Association.*

Though by far the most spectacular of these are the Monterey cypress and Monterey pine communities of the Monterey Peninsula, these have been photographed so much and are so well known all over the world, that I thought it best to show here one of the lesser known of these little forests, made up of bishop and beach pines and Mendocino cypresses on the Mendocino Coast. The Mendocino cypresses do not appear in this kind of exposed position, but are generally found down in the hollows and the little canyons. The two kinds of pine are told apart by the bishop pine's having two rigid dark yellowish green needles in a bundle, while the beach pine (a blood brother of the lodgepole pine) has two very dark green and slender needles in a bundle, bark covered with either yellow or purple scales, and light yellowish brown cones. The nearby Mendocino cypress, of course, is easily identified by its very dark and dull green leaves being closely wrapped around the twiglets. During the winter rains the cypresses, apparently liking plenty of water, are often found in flooded places.

Monterey Cypress

There is one place on the Mendocino Coast, called the White Plains, where the white sandstone rock forms a strange layer that prevents any water from settling, and these three trees, plus the giant chinquapin, there become queerly stunted dwarf trees, rarely more than three feet high.

On the Monterey Peninsula, of course, the Monterey cypresses present almost as strange an appearance, being twisted by the strong sea wind and the lash of the salt spray into all kinds of odd forms, with odder flat hat tops tilted at still odder angles, and usually decorated by two weird growths, a dripping gray "moss" that is actually a lichen (made up of both an alga and a fungus), and a strange orange-colored alga. This latter covers some of the twigs with cobweblike, rusty, felt-feeling, fungal masses that glow against the sunset as if they had inner lights of their own. These trees and the Monterey pines often make gloomy thickets, out of which you can peer at the sun shining on the blue Pacific Ocean as if looking out from a cave of darkness into a region of paradise.

Beach Pine

The Sitka Spruce Forest

The true rain forests of the Pacific Coast of Washington and British Columbia have as much as 144 inches of rain a year or even more, or as much as most tropical jungles. This forms the last really extensive virgin wilderness in

Sitka spruce rain forest of northwest Washington.—*Photo by Kenneth S. Brown. Courtesy American Forest Products Industries, Inc.*

Sitka Spruce

the United States, and most of it lies within the Olympic Peninsula, mainly in Olympic National Park, being repeated again to the north in British Columbia.

Sitka spruce is monarch of this forest, rising even above the Douglas fir to heights as tall as 280 feet and girths of 10 or 12 feet wide or more. Other great trees, such as the noble fir, western red cedar, and western hemlocks, stand about in humble deferment. Seldom do you find such fine straight trunks, lustrous dark reddish brown or deep purple in color, without a branch for a hundred feet or more, as is found with the Sitka spruce. The dark green but white-banded needles stand up so stiffly around the branchlets that they seem like rows of soldiers at attention. And even the branches sweep grandly up to the sky, in the manner of an ancient king, lifting arms to pray to his god, the cone-tipped branchlets hanging down like bracelets dripping jewels. At the bottom the trunks are strengthened with great bracing fluted flanges that are very necessary, considering that the rain-soaked ground below could become dangerously unstable.

The western red cedar, or canoe cedar, with its bark ranging from stringy to fibrous and from bright cinnamon red to grayish brown, and its dark yellowish green scaly leaves, wrapping tightly around the twiglets, is another exciting giant, but one wound deeply into the lives of the ancient Indians of this coast. Large cedars were hewed down with stone or horn axes, and then cut and burned hollow to make great canoes, some over 60 feet long and capable of 200-mile ocean voyages after whales. Other trees were carved as logs into the marvelously intricate totem poles, some actually as much as a hundred feet high after the Indians got steel tools. Other trees were cut into timber to make the huge potlach halls for celebration, feasting, and displaying riches. And the bark was used for everything from baby diapers and bedding to the strongest kind of cordage or rope.

Damp and quiet are these great rain forests, carpeted below with many ferns and lovely, pale, elfin flowers. Lichens hang from the tree branches like beards of patriarchs, and moss is everywhere on trunk and branch and fallen giant. Your feet sink deeply into leaf mold that tells of centuries upon centuries of leaf fall, and out of the silence comes the drawn-out, quavering, eerie whistles of the varied thrush from where the sunlight strikes so far above, unseen below. There is little animal and bird life here, but you stand in the midst of tree life immemorially ancient and grand.

CHAPTER EIGHT

Understanding the Leaf-dropping Forests

THE DECIDUOUS FORESTS east of the Rockies and those found from the Rockies to the Pacific Coast each have their special glories. The leaf-dropping forests of the East are unsurpassed for the variety of trees they contain and for the spectacular colors of their foliage in autumn. Although our western deciduous forests do not have the variety of our eastern woodlands, they provide welcome oases of shade, often in hot, desert surroundings, and furnish food and shelter to many small animals.

DECIDUOUS FORESTS EAST OF THE ROCKIES

It is sad that so much of the great and ancient deciduous forest of eastern North America has gone under the axe and into the earth torn by the plow, but the part that still remains stands as a precious heritage and a future strength that we should try to improve with all our power. This is, without doubt, the premier deciduous forest of the whole earth, the most varied and unique in species, the most lively in the way it handles sunlight and the wind-dancing of leaves, the most lovely in flowers, and the most remarkable in the varied and unusual uses for its wood, bark, fruit, and seeds. By opening your eyes and ears, and even using your nose, as you should in studying this or any forest, you can embark on one of the most refreshing and interesting adventures possible.

It is the fall, of course, when this forest comes to its greatest glory, the world of the woods seeming to come alive under the touch of a master painter, recklessly but skillfully decking the trees with many a marvelous tint and shade of scarlet, yellow, orange, and purple. Yet this is actually a sign to us of death, for the trees have heard the warning of the coming winter in the touch of the first chill breezes coming down from the northland. Slowly they tighten the cork noose that hides itself at the base of each leaf until the day comes when the sap no longer runs up the thin pipes of the cambial layer to bring water and minerals for the leaf to manufacture into plant material and food. The noose around each leaf has been tied tight and death must now come. But what a glorious death and a promise of a glorious new birth in the following spring! The dead leaf, deprived quickly of its green chlorophyll, which dissolves as if it had never been, now shows its long-hidden crystals of red and yellow, pink and scarlet, purple or orange or tan pigments that give it new beauty. The sugar maple probably most fully symbolizes the loveliness of an eastern fall; the acid soil is partly responsible for the brightest colors of the leaves. Flame red of fire, yellow light of sunlight, orange of sunset gleam and sparkle in the sugar maple leaf, and twirl with it down to the earth in a turning kaleidoscope of colors so that the earth beneath these maple trees becomes a carpet from the Arabian nights. But the great calm golden light of the beech, like a halo about this great tree, the blazing, dancing scarlet of scarlet oak and red maple, and the rich purple of the leaves of the ash are also vital parts of this deciduous tree symphony of universal beauty. They tell us a story of rich soil, of acid from the soil bringing crystals to sharp color, of trees that, through long eons of time, have developed a method to escape the attacks of cold on life and retire into their wood-insulated hearts and roots until the freezing days are past. Some of the typical colors of these woods are shown in the accompanying simple chart.

Sugar Maple

Beech

Scarlet Oak

Some Colors of Fall Trees in the East

Red	Yellow	Tan	Purple	Scarlet	Red-orange-yellow
Scarlet oak	Poplar	White oak	Beech	Red maple	Sugar maple
Sweet gum	Birch		mahogany	Scarlet oak	
Red maple	Beech		Ash	Dogwood	
Sumac	Tulip tree		Wild prune	Sassafras	
Dogwood	Willow			Redbud	
				Sweet gum	
				Blueberry	
				Sumac	

Red Maple

TYPICAL EASTERN DECIDUOUS WOODLAND

To walk quietly through these woods, to pause and linger for awhile studying something you find or see of great beauty, to run in a burst of sudden joy along a woodland trail—these are the delightful hours. For these are the trees of singing birds and hopping, running, climbing animals, far more than the darker and more somber, quiet coniferous forests. Here, the leaves of the quaking aspen, turning and twisting, fluttering and whispering with every slightest breeze, are only one of many kinds of trees whose foliage dances and sings with the wind in a light and lithesome way. So also do the leaves of the maples and the elms, the birches and the ashes. Here are the woods of a thousand uses for man—maples telling you of their sweet sugary sap; ashes with their straight and limber wood that promises both bows and fine arrows; hickory, rough and tough and hard, with the strength to make the best tool handles or the strongest bows; oak for luxurious tables and chairs; sassafras with its healing red tea; a thousand wild plums, cherries, raspberries, and blackberries to delight your meals; then the nuts from the beeches, oaks, walnuts, pecans, and hickories.

And here we should mention the American chestnut, but sadly, for once this great tree, with its delicious brown nuts, ranged through most of the eastern deciduous forests, showing its creamy blossoms in springtime to make a white sea of flowers over the miles of forest tops. But now it is largely gone, killed by the chestnut blight, a horrible fungus disease brought from China. For years the whitened skeletons blighted thousands of square miles of eastern forest, but, at last, they have sunk softly into the earth and the ugliness has gone.

In the East today the dominant trees include the great white oak, king of trees; the tall tulip tree; the smooth, gray-barked beech; the glorious sugar, silver, and red maples; the yellow and canoe birches, and the basswood. An occasional white pine or eastern hemlock gives the dark touch of the conifers, and sometimes some pitch pines grow in the clearings made by man or fire. Some of the lesser trees that form the lower stories in this forest are the redbud, the dogwood, the sassafras, sourwood, black gum, box elder, black locust, black haw, hornbeam, and eastern ironwood, assisted by such lowly bushes as the witch hazel and chokecherry.

Both flowers and leaves tell us stories about trees. The tulip tree, with its great many-petaled, many-stamened, many-pistiled blossoms, is a sign of ancient times and primitive beginnings, for it is a member of the magnolias, among the most ancient deciduous trees on earth. Yet, despite its primitive nature, it is one of our most successful trees, possibly because of its great height, sometimes up to two hundred feet and beyond, which allows it to find light for its leaves high in the air above the proudest oaks and maples below.

We can also tell the tulip trees and their cousin magnolias by their primitive shape as revealed in a few large branches and scarcely any small branches or

Black Haw

Tulip Tree

Sweetbay Magnolia

Autumn deciduous forest woods in New Hampshire, with birches, maples, beeches, ashes, etc.—*Photo by Eric M. Sanford. Courtesy Alpha Photo Associates, Inc.*

twigs. Their smooth-sided simple leaves are another sign of simple beginnings. Certain other trees have characteristics that hit you immediately when you see them closely, such as the very smooth, grayish blue bark of even the largest beech tree; the deeply grooved reddish brown bark of the sassafras, aromatic in smell and contrasting sharply with its bright green twigs, or the gleaming white bark of the paper birch, with its dark brown triangular-shaped lenticels or branch scars. Then there are the very thick evergreen leaves of the mountain laurel, a lower-story tree; the innumerable small leaflets of the honey locust, which indicate a very advanced tree, evolutionarily speaking, each group of leaflets arranged in pyramids and with dangerous-looking triple thorns at their bases; the key-shaped fruits of the maples, which tell us of long voyages on the winds of fall, and many others. We can tell how primitive or advanced a tree is by what point it lies between the primitive, smooth-sided leaves of the magnolia, the medium-advanced toothed leaves of the oak, and the far-advanced division of a leaf into many tiny leaflets of the honey locust.

Mountain Laurel

Honey Locust

COVE-TYPE APPALACHIAN HARDWOOD FORESTS

Drive into the Appalachian Mountains and you see the dark crests of the red spruce and balsam fir forests far above you, telling of the days when the glaciers pushed south and most of these mountains were covered with this kind of northern and cold-loving forest. But in the lower, deep-shaded, protected coves, or canyons, as westerners would call them, strange collections of trees tell a different story.

Though mixed with many more modern plants, these hermitlike coves include the ancient hardwood cove trees, as well as shrubs and herbs that once stretched continuously through a warm, almost subtropical climate, from America to Asia. Included in these knights of the past are the American hornbeam, the ironwood or eastern hop hornbeam, the magnolias and tulip tree, the sassafras, witch hazel, the wood anemone, and several others.

American Hornbeam

The interesting thing about the cove forests is their great variety of species in a comparatively small area, without any one or two trees being dominant as in the oak-hickory forests, or the spruce-fir forest. These cove woods tell us of the way the ancient forests were long ago before certain species began to become more successful than others. Protected in these hidden coves in the Appalachians, the ancient diverse-species forests continue (see photo).

Probably the most common trees of the cove hardwood forests, though nowhere is the collection of trees in these coves always the same, are the white basswood, sweet buckeye, tulip tree, sugar maple, yellow birch, beech, and eastern hemlock. Slightly less abundant are the bitternut hickory, red oak, white oak, and cucumber magnolia. Underneath are found such smaller trees and shrubs as the big rhododendron, mountain silver bell, box elder, mountain laurel, sourwood, yellow gum, umbrella tree, mountain maple, and the flowering dogwood.

Sweet Buckeye

Throughout the Appalachians, as if they were museum islands, preserving precious relics from all over, we find not only these interesting coves, but also tree associations that remind us of other areas. Thus, oaks and hickories on dry ridge tops bring to mind the comparatively dry midwestern forests, while a collection of beeches, maples, and hemlocks on a north-facing slope makes us think of the borders of the eastern Great Lakes, and, of course, the red spruce and

Cove-type hardwood forest in mountains of North Carolina, including (from left to right in foreground) sugar maple, hickory, and buckeye.—*Photo courtesy U.S. Department of Agriculture.*

balsam fir of the highest peaks remind us of the great dark north woods. But the coves are the most successful examples of microclimates preserved for so many millions of years by the protecting arms of the mountains that they seem to almost go back to the times of the dinosaurs with similar tree groupings.

WOODLOTS OF EASTERN AND MIDWESTERN FARMS

Though the great days of the widespread deciduous forests are gone in eastern and midwestern America, the giving up by farmers of the marginal lands

Forest in Maryland uplands, including oaks, tulip tree, hickories, sassafras, sweet gum, sourwood, black cherry, butternut, etc.—*Photo courtesy U.S. Department of Agriculture.*

to the wild, and the greater interest in farming trees among small landowners has brought a resurgence of woodlands to many areas where man's axe, plow, and fire had once swept most of the trees away. If it were not for the encroaching of cities and suburbs, this return to the woods would be even more widespread, offering greater opportunities for recreation and beauty. Indeed, many farmers are realizing that leafy woods and hedgerows offer shelter and nesting places for our many bird allies who fight the caterpillars, grasshoppers, leaf bugs, and other pests of garden and field.

Yellow Birch

In hedgerows and woodlots, abandoned fields and dying orchards, the small, quick-growing trees are springing up to strengthen the soil. In the East they include the birches, blackjack or scrub oak, Virginia or scrub pine, sassafras and eastern red cedar among the larger species, and the wild cherries, staghorn sumac, dogwood, crab apples, hawthorns, wild plums, and others among the small trees and shrubs. In the Midwest are most of these, except the cedar, and scrub oaks and pines, but also the crab apples, chockecherries, and serviceberries, as well as scrub hickories, cottonwoods, aspens, and butternuts (see photo of midwestern woodlot). If only the farmers would keep their cows and other stock from overgrazing these small woods (see The Results of Overgrazing in Chapter 5), these young forests would begin to re-create much that was beautiful and of interest as in the days of old.

Chokecherry

The Adventurous Hawthorns

Most people do not recognize the hawthorns that are often common in these regenerated woods, because they seem to copy so many other small trees in appearance. In fact they are often called "no-name trees." Though only experts can differentiate between the literally hundreds of different species of hawthorns, you can almost immediately tell a hawthorn from all similar trees by finding most of the following characteristics: (1) cut a small branch and trim a piece of it open down the middle and you will see in cross section that the pith is solid, perfectly round, and plain (unlike other trees that have starlike piths or ones with numerous flanges or diaphragms or that are hollow in the middle);

Hawthorn

Woodlot on farm in southern Wisconsin, with such trees as oaks, hickories, red maple, ashes, wild plum, crab apple, chokecherry, hawthorns, etc.—*Photo courtesy U.S. Forest Service.*

(2) the leaves are generally well toothed on their edges and often deeply indented (a sign of an advanced-type tree); (3) there is a true lateral thorn at the base of each branchlet; (4) the fruits are small and applelike with bony centers.

The hawthorns, as we have already noted, are particularly interesting, because they belong in an advanced class of very adventurous and changeable new trees that are springing up everywhere on man-destroyed lands. How they adapt themselves to these new strange environments is worthy of our study, wonder, and encouragement, for they bring green beauty into many wasted and hurt places.

MAIN CENTRAL STATES DECIDUOUS GROVES AND FORESTS

As we move westward from the Appalachians, we come into gradually dryer areas, halfway, more or less, between the damp warm air brought up from the Gulf of Mexico in the South and the damp cold air that comes down from the Great Lakes in the North. It is an area that, for millions of years, has seen a series of battles and skirmishes between the prairie grasses and midwestern deciduous forests. In this war the grasses have sometimes won and spread over wide areas where the dry climate increased, while wet periods have seen the forests occupying most of the region. The Indians in their days helped the forests against the grassy prairies by burning the grass every year to help their hunting and planting. The white man has cut down the area of both of these former widespread plant communities by plowing under the grass to plant crops and also cutting down many of the trees to make way for farms or to use for lumber. The forests of this area, largely made up of dominant oaks and hickories, show a liking for more sunlight than the eastern, southern, and northern forests; midwestern forests have far fewer mosses, liverworts, mushrooms, and ferns in their undergrowth than the other forests.

Oak-Hickory and Beech-Maple Forests

Both oaks and hickories are very adaptable trees, but both seem to grow best where it is neither too damp nor too dry. Beeches and maples tend to prefer

Northern Red Oak

Southern Red Oak

Shellbark Hickory

Oak-hickory association in Midwest.—*Courtesy State of Illinois Department of Conservation.*

dampness, and so are inclined to be more eastern, northern, or southern in population spread. The oaks and hickories, though common in the East, reach their most notable numbers and growth in the Midwest. Both are noted for their very fine hardwood, though the hickory is far tougher and so used mostly for tool handles, while the oak goes into fine cabinetwork, floors, and furniture.

White Oak

THE RICH OAKS AND THEIR POOR RELATIVES　　Where oak and hickory are dominant, they set their distinctive stamp on the kinds of wood they live in and its sign language. Oaks can be divided into two major groups: the rich oaks—such as the white, bur, pin and northern red oaks, which prefer deep, rich, but generally well-drained soils—and their poor relations—the post, black, chestnut, scarlet, and blackjack oaks, which might like this kind of soil, but are forced by their poorer growth habits or other characteristics to live on the poorer, dryer, or more fire-damaged soils. The latter group cannot stand up to the competition of the bigger, stronger trees and are forced out of the bottomlands into the rocks, hills, and sands. However, the poor relations have a very important job to do, that is, to make the soil richer in the poorer areas, or to stabilize erosion areas or sand dunes, as the blackjack oak and black oaks do on the Indiana dunes. Watch for all of these oaks and remember that each gives us a sign of the kind of land in which it lives.

Post Oak

It is actually more interesting to watch for these poorer oaks and study them, as they are vital adventurers and land regainers in the borderlands of combat with erosion and the damage done by fire and man. Thus, first grass and herbs move into an area of poor or rocky soil or a burnt-over area and put down a thin layer of soil; then bushes follow, and, after them, the first of these oaks or similar trees (see Secondary Plant Succession in Chapter 6). Study the roots and see how they must scrabble and grab into the very thin soil cover to take hold in a way that the richer, more climax-type oaks would never deign to do. The latter wait until a good job of soil-making is done before their seedlings begin to grow. In the end, of course, it is the great oaks, hickories, and other dominant trees that will rule the land.

The climax or dominant oaks of this forest have their unique characteristics. The white oak is the most massive of them all with a tremendous templelike spread of branches. The bur oak is instantly recognized by the furry, burrlike appearances of its acorns. The northern red oak has dark brown, smooth bark and acorns with very shallow cups. The pin oak shows many tiny, pinlike branches that come out of the main ones.

Shagbark Hickory

THE RICH HICKORIES AND THEIR POOR RELATIONS　　The hickories are also divided into rich trees and their poor relations. The shagbark hickory, easily told by its wide shreds of bark, and the shellbark hickory, with the bark coming off in shell-like plates, are the great trees of good soil. But the red hickory, with its slightly ridged gray bark; the mockernut hickory, characterized by densely hairy leaflets; and the bitternut hickory, with its comparatively smooth gray bark and bitter-tasting nuts, are trees that find their best homes on poor soil. The hickories, unlike the oaks, with the exception of the gracefully thin pin oak, have a straight main trunk with much smaller side branches, forming an oval shape.

Other trees that are found in the midwestern deciduous forests include the beech, sugar maple, black cherry, American ash, linden, sweet locust, and the yellow birch. Common lesser trees of the understory are the redbud, flowering

Mockernut Hickory

Shagbark hickory.—*Photo courtesy Ontario Department of Lands and Forests.*

Beech-maple climax forest, showing understory of young beech trees, in North Chagrin Reservation, near Cleveland, Ohio.—*Courtesy Cleveland Museum of Natural History.*

dogwood, sourwood, box elder, black locust, sweet gum, black haw, hornbeam, eastern ironwood, crab apple, witch hazel, and chokecherry.

Groves of the Midwest Prairies and Great Plains

For centuries on centuries the bur oak has left the shelter of the main oak-hickory forest and moved out onto the prairies to become the premier tree of what the pioneers called "the prairie groves" or "oak openings." These clusters of trees in the midst of grasslands seem on hot summer days the essence of coolness and shade, with their great oaks bowing their huge limbs outward in benign shelter over the land. To the pioneers, it was heaven indeed to come with sweat-rivuled bodies through the hot prairies and find in the shelter of these oaks not only cooling shade, but what seemed more like a park than a forest because of the absence of much undergrowth.

Bur Oak

Though the bur oaks completely dominate these woods, they usually have with them such trees as the shagbark hickory, the sweet locust, white ash, white elm, and American linden. Beneath these giants are a few lesser trees, such as the black haw, red haw, hackberry, and cottonwood. Actually, the climate in these oak groves has been becoming moister through recent years, so that, if left alone, they would eventually turn into a climax forest of walnut, hickory, ash, oak, and linden. Today, indeed, the bur oaks are advancing into the grasslands, and the armies of the grass are slowly retreating before the trees, except where man interferes with his plowing and cutting. You find signs of this advance wherever a young oak tree, or associated species, is found growing out in the edge of the prairie.

White Elm

Cottonwood and Aspen Groves of the Northern Great Plains

The Sioux Indians called both the aspen and the cottonwood the "wagichuns," or "talking trees," because of the voice of the wind playing through

Bur oak in Simcoe County, Ontario.—*Photo courtesy Ontario Department of Lands and Forests.*

Cottonwood and aspen grove on Great Plains of Montana, in a blaze of yellow autumn leaves.—*Photo courtesy American Forest Products Industries, Inc.*

Trembling Aspen

Eastern Cottonwood

their easily shaken leaves. In a good wind the aspens laugh and titter, and they hiss and whisper when their small leaves dance and flash like mirrors in the sun, while the cottonwoods seem to have a little deeper liquid sound of gurgling and rattling. Since these trees are nearly always a sign of water being near, and water is very precious in the dry West, the Indians also said they were sacred trees, especially sacred to the Great Spirit, and that, if you listened long enough, you might hear His voice.

In the prairie states of Canada these groves often grow much bigger than in the United States, forming real forests to northward, seeming to foreshadow the great dark spruce and fir forests that stretch toward the Pole. In these groves many birds find their homes—the woodpeckers first, including red-headed woodpeckers and sapsuckers, often making holes in the trees for nests, particularly the cottonwoods, whose wood is softer and whose heartwood usually begins to decay after fifty years of growth. In time the bluebirds, starlings, owls, and others borrow the use of these holes until a grove may have hundreds of homes for a dozen different species. Because these woods grow so rapidly and their lives are so brief by other tree standards, rarely reaching a hundred years, they are perfectly adapted to enriching and holding the soil against erosion in as short a tree time as possible—vital factors where the heavy rains of great thunderheads thrash the ground each summer with soil-destroying force.

In the long-gone days the buffalo, antelope, and Indians of the wild plains came to rest in the shade of these trees, and their ghosts may still talk among the leaves. It is still possible to find the Silence here and see the bigness of a clear blue sky, to watch the violet green swallows dart and swoop after insects, and feel the warm winds coming across hundreds of miles of open plains.

SOUTHERN SWAMPS AND THE TROPICAL FOREST

The Cypress Swamps

The southeastern and southern bald cypress and southern white cedar swamps are as near to jungles as we get in most of North America, outside of the southern tip of Florida. Both trees occur in almost pure stands, or, sometimes, a scattering of cedars may be found associated with the cypresses. But a number of trees may be associated with both, particularly on their fringes, including swamp cottonwood, swamp chestnut oak, scarlet and red maples, loblolly and slash pines, overcup and live oaks, sweet bay, black tupelo, and the red bay persea. Sometimes an understory of smaller trees and bushes occurs, including inkberry, swamp cyrilla, poison sumac, hornbeam, yaupon, and buttonbush, ringed with cattails, rushes, and sedges. Beyond in the open water grow such plants as pond lilies, golden club, water hyacinth, quillwort, and bladderwort. To the south the cabbage palmetto palms ring the waters of these swamps.

Southern White Cedar

Swamp country is strange and beautiful, though too often made unpleasant by mosquitoes and other biting bugs that require the carrying of a good repellent. Strange is the sound of huge bubbles of gas rising up through the muck and muddy water to explode with a soggy plop that suggests the breathing of some

Florida bald cypress swamp.—*Photo courtesy U.S. Forest Service.*

Bald Cypress

underwater monster. The bald cypress itself is probably the strangest tree found in the swamp. The queer, fibrous, scaly bark peels off in long, thin, reddish brown strips, and the "knees" of peculiarly hollow hard wood that grow up around the tree's base and are attached to the spreading root system conjure up thoughts of a tree from some place like Mars or Venus. The peculiar "sinkers," around which the root system is formed, apparently act as vital supports to hold the great weight of the tree upright in what is a very shaky underpinning of soil. The leaves of this conifer fall off in winter—a sign of some peculiar situation because this is very rare in conifers. The most logical suggestion I have heard is that it is because the leaves operate during most of the year to send down oxygen to roots that have none because of the water and decaying material that surrounds them, but are not needed for this in winter when the tree is dormant. Evidently the root-growing enzymes need this oxygen in order to operate.

SWAMP WILDLIFE   Most of the year these swamps seethe with all kinds of life, especially insects, which swarm everywhere, and a great variety of birds that wade, hunt, and fly in every part. The low, hoarse croaks of the great blue heron and the brilliantly white American egret sound from deep within the swamps while the black-crowned night heron calls its flat-sounding "quaark!" in the warm evening, and the American bittern pumps out a slow, deep "oonk-ga-chunk," like a huge man driving a pile, from the mysterious shadows. In the most southerly swamps alligators may appear like innocent logs floating on the waters, but they have cruel-toothed jaws and spiny tails that can swing like a flail if a rabbit or deer comes near.

INSECT-EATING SWAMP PLANTS   Among the queerest forms of vibrant life in the steaming hothouse of a summer swamp—and one with special meaning for us—are the insect-eating plants, such as the Dutchman's-pipe, the sundew, the Venus flytrap, and others, some found also in northern swamps and bogs. These deceptively innocent living things wait quietly for insects to come to them for nectar or because of the fetid smell some give forth. The Dutchman's-pipe allows its insect guests to walk down its slippery walls, lined with down-sloping hairs, into a parlor from which there is usually no escape. The fact that a mosquito lays its eggs in the water found in the Dutchman's-pipe and that the mosquitoes that hatch do escape has been used as an argument against any meat-absorbing on the part of these plants. But why the elaborate passageway with the down-facing hairs? Also, such plants are always found in nitrogen-lacking soil and water, a lack the insects, when absorbed, can make up.

EPIPHYTES   Epiphytes, a plant feature common also to tropical jungles, are found in the swamps. One of these is called "Spanish moss" and does look like a yellow green hanging moss on the branches of the cypresses, but is really a trailing plant, or ephiphyte, which uses the tree only for support while aerial roots tap moisture and minerals from the moist air without need to go into the ground. Other epiphytes look like dark clumps high in the trees, but can always be told from the similar-appearing mistletoes by the long hanging roots below them.

Subtropical and Tropical Forests of Florida and Louisiana

Subtropical forests of a sort range from the Carolinas and Florida along the Gulf Coast to Texas, but they are most genuinely subtropical in Florida, where

A subtropical hammock at Highlands Hammock State Park, Florida, showing Sabal palmetto, live oak, laurel oak, and sweet gum.—*Photo courtesy Florida Board of Parks.*

there are areas in the south that see practically no frost. One good sign of these woods is the Sabal palmetto or palm, shown in the photograph. Other dominant trees are the live oak, laurel oak, and sweet gum, which raise their heads above the palms, but don't seem to drown them out with shade. It is not as dense or junglelike as the next-described forest.

MANGROVE SWAMPS   A true tropical jungle exists along the southern edge of Florida, though minus the jaguars, boa constrictors, and other strange animals of the jungles of Central and South America. The jungle starts on the edge of the sea, where the mangrove swamps, inhabited by strange half-marine, half-land plants, are actually building land out into the sea by collecting mud, silt, and sand brought in by the waves and holding it around the networks of stiltlike roots the mangroves put down on the water's edge. The round, leathery berry or fruit has a single seed, which peculiarly germinates inside the fruit, producing a heavy, dartlike stem, which, when the seed is dropped, causes it to sink itself immediately into the mud. From the upper end green leafy shoots spring up like magic. This is a very unusual adaptation to this sea-edge habitat and explains part of the success of these sea-swamp trees.

True tropical jungle in Collier-Seminole State Park, Florida.—*Photo courtesy Florida Board of Parks.*

Laurel Oak

In time, as the mangroves work out to sea, other trees begin to follow, building real land as they come, because they are protected from the waves by the mangroves. This jungle is very thick, with an interwoven underbrush and hanging lianas or tropical vines that make it nearly impossible to penetrate save with a big knife or axe. The bewildering number of trees of the jungle have strange names and often strange characteristics. A few of the tallest, those who provide the top canopy, include the Florida strangler fig, which first climbs on other trees as a vine until it strangles and kills one and then takes its place in the forest; the paradise tree, so named because of its beautiful yellow flowers and purple or scarlet fruits; the gumbo-limbo, with papery red bark made up of birchlike scales; the slash pine, already met with; the Simpson nakedwood, with fragrant flowers covered with white silken hairs; the jungle plum or false mastic, with yellow, thick, juicy, one-seeded fruits; and the Bahama strongbark, with orange red, cherrylike fruits.

Slash Pine

Smaller trees and shrubs appear below this top canopy, including the Florida poison tree, or poisonwood, whose sap is extremely poisonous to the touch; pond apple; Bahama Lysiloma; Florida fishpoison tree, or Jamaica dogwood, which has a poison in the bark used by Indians to stupefy fish; satinleaf, with its leaves lustrous bluish green above and with coppery satin hairs below; the geiger tree, and many others.

In this jungle the struggle of life against life is more apparent than in our northern forests. Every bit of space seems to be fought for in this lush growth where aerial as well as regular roots seek food for the plants that own them. The strangler fig emphasizes the extreme of this struggle, by starting as a small vine winding up a large tree towards the light and ending by actually killing the tree it has climbed.

SOUTHERN RIVER-BOTTOM FORESTS

Sycamore

These thick forests, with two of our largest eastern trees, the tulip tree and the sycamore, towering above them, also include many fighters over the rich soil laid down by waters of countless years from the great rivers of the South. The farthest northern arm of this dark, thick forest reaches up to where the Ohio

Southern river-bottom forest in Georgia, including tulip tree mixed with other hardwoods.—*Photo courtesy School of Forestry, University of Georgia.*

touches southern Illinois. In this forest are primitive trees as well as more advanced ones. We have already noted the primitive nature of the tulip tree (see How to Tell Primitive from Advanced Trees in Chapter 7). The great sycamores, where allowed to grow, sometimes reach 170 feet or more into the air, with trunks as much as 14 feet in diameter, and show the primitive characteristics of bark which flakes off in large irregular patches to make way for new growth, as well as great limbs which are almost bare of small side limbs. The flaking of the bark, exposing different layers below, produces the strange and beautiful design of white, greenish, tan, and light gray mottling.

Other climax trees that rim the top of the forest with their leaves are the red maple; the river birch; the bald cypress; the overcup oak, and other oaks such as the willow, water, swamp red, and swamp chestnut oaks; large cottonwoods, and the wahoo elm. Most are characterized by powerful root systems, used to hold them in place against the powerful pull of floods, and to hold the good soil beneath them at the same time. Look for the signs on the bark of these trees of where the last flood came and left its drying mud or other debris.

Under the great trees are lower canopies of such small trees and shrubs as the sugarberry; pawpaw, with its enormous 3- to 5-inch-long yellow and tropical-looking berry; box elder; rusty black haw; various hawthorns; hackberry; wild black cherry; poison sumac; sweet gum; redbud; black gum, with its vicious spines; water locust, and many others. The pawpaw is evidently a sign of a time when warmer climates existed in these parts than do now, together with a true tropical forest, but the pawpaw is a tropical tree that has learned to survive winter frosts.

River Birch

Water Oak

NORTHEASTERN AND MIDWESTERN STREAMSIDE WOODLANDS

The waters may be cold, but we need to ask also: are they clear? Wherever they are really crystal clear, this is a sign to us that the woods upstream are in good shape and holding in the soil. We can confidently walk up that stream into

Streamside woodland in New England, with willows, alders, and other water-loving plants.—*Photo courtesy American Museum of Natural History.*

Black Willow

Pussy Willow

Black Ash

Red Ash

wilderness and beauty where the balance of life is being maintained. But if the waters are muddy or have other trash in them, something is very wrong up that stream, either man-made or fire-made. If we investigate and find out what it is—and it is usually a place where destruction of the forest has caused erosion—we can tell those in authority about it and perhaps help correct it. For mud and trash in any stream gives us a dark warning, a warning of danger to all America.

Moving from north to south in eastern Canada and the states below it, we can often tell fairly closely where we are by the trees that line a stream. In Quebec and northern New England the likely trees by the streams are canoe birch and arborvitae; the red and silver maples; willows such as the Bebb, black, and pussy willows; and the black and red ash. Farther south, in central Pennsylvania, the arborvitae and canoe birch have disappeared, as has the black ash, and the eastern cottonwood has become common, but the maples continue. From Maine south, the sycamore becomes a major tree, particularly along slow streams. Red ash, by the way, is always a sign of water being close by, no matter where it is found, which is not always true of the other trees.

Smaller trees and bushes found along streams and rivers in both areas are the witch hazel, hornbeams, and flowering dogwood (which does not appear in Canada). In the South the rhododendrons become common along mountain streams.

There are few things more delightful than to listen to the rustle and gurgle of water on a warm day in the eastern woodlands, and rest your eyes with green of leaves and the contrasting but warm brown, gray, and reddish brown colors of the tree trunks. Sift out the scents that come to you on the wind and you are likely to catch the pungent wintergreen aroma of the leaves and bark of the cherry birch. You can tell also the similar but weaker aroma of the yellow birch, but the two are much more quickly distinguished by noticing the magnificently gleaming mahogany red bark of the cherry birch, so different from the dull yellowish brown or reddish brown bark of the yellow birch. Notice that both the birches and the maples have winged seeds, those of the maple looking like tiny propellers, those of the birch like butterflies. These are the signs of trees that have developed a very efficient method of spreading their seeds far and wide, whirled off in spinning flight by strong winds in the fall, often for miles.

In the Middle West the forest surrounding the streamside woodlands is somewhat dryer than farther east, and this seems to make even the woods near the stream different in feeling too. The great sycamore is here of course, especially along the rivers, where the river birch too is common, at least as far north as Ohio and southern Wisconsin. But the river birch completely avoids the swift streams and mountain rills liked by its cousins. Another tree preferring slow-moving streams is the eastern cottonwood, which is midwestern in habitat, more than eastern. It and the sycamore are often the dominant trees by the rivers in bottomland midwestern forests, as shown in the accompanying photo. Still another tree liking the slow-moving streams of the Midwest is the box elder, actually another maple. But the plebeian, plain-looking, often short-topped, short-lived and unobtrusive box elder is also a very beloved and useful tree farther west, where it shades the river banks in the hot Great Plains along with the cottonwoods, and also spreads into dry, poor-soiled places where few other trees of that region like to go and there helps the soil to grow. It is an eager adapter and adventurer among trees. Other common trees along the midwestern streams are the silver and red maples, American elm, and the white, red, and

Flood plain forest in Ohio on Rocky River with cottonwood-sycamore association.—
Photo courtesy Cleveland Museum of Natural History.

blue ashes (the white ash being renowned as the source of wood for baseball bats).

DECIDUOUS FORESTS OF THE WEST

White Ash

STREAMSIDE WOODLANDS

There are often too many different kinds of leaves talking in the deciduous woodlands of the Midwest and East to hear one kind alone, but in the West from the Rockies to the Pacific you usually hear only two or three at most. The light, fast chatter of the quaking aspens is heard high in the mountains; the liquid, mocking rustle of the cottonwoods by the desert streams. The cottonwoods team with the long sigh of the willows and pretty lisping of the alders along the Pacific Coast streams. The only exception to this rule is found among the streams of the far Northwest, where the greater rainfall produces a greater proliferation of species, including Oregon ashes, the Pacific dogwood, the water birch, and a few other trees.

Black Cottonwood

The peace, shade, and coolness of a streamside woodland in the intermountain west is greatly accentuated by the generally desert surroundings. With the heat of the sun blazing down on the surrounding sagebrush, creosote bush, or cacti, a river, with its cottonwoods and willows (see photo), is indeed a green and rustling oasis where the weary desert traveler can lie in the shade, watch the blue sky and the trembling leaves above him and forget his troubles.

In California and Arizona the California sycamore, short-trunked and heavy, spreads its octopuslike arms skyward by the larger slow-moving streams and gives a feeling of strength to a quiet summer day. Its leaves are such a light yellowish green that they seem almost like a part of the light of the sun, but they do give shade. The power of this tree to grow in poor, rocky soil and to withstand floods makes it very valuable in saving streambanks and other work in flood control.

Western Sycamore

Cottonwoods and willows along a desert river in Nevada.—*Photo courtesy U.S. Forest Service.*

Water Birch

staminate

pistillate

Red Alder

Some western streams dry up around both sycamores and cottonwoods; so these trees are not invariably good indicators of water present, but trees that always reveal the presence of water are the water birch, with very wide and well-toothed leaves and found in both the Rockies and the Pacific Northwest, and the red, white, and other alders, with their somewhat narrower-toothed leaves, all along the Pacific Coast. These trees grow only when and where water is running very close by throughout the year. Willows are not persnickety like this, but will grow along streams that go dry in summer. Willows show signs of being very active in their evolution because they have so many species difficult to distinguish, like the hawthorns. About the only easy one to tell is the valley willow of California, Arizona, and southern Nevada, whose twigs snap off easily and cleanly at the base when bent. This is the sign of a tree that has developed a good way to spread itself in floods, as the snapped off twigs may land in a sandbar far below and start growing into new trees.

California fan palms in Palm Canyon near Palm Springs, California.—*Photo courtesy U.S. Forest Service.*

On the really hot, dry deserts of southwestern Arizona and southeastern California, the most distinctive streamside trees are the strange and beautiful California fan palms (see photo). These palms, with their great clusters of live fanlike leaves above, and the long hulalike dresses of dead leaves hanging below, gather wherever there is enough shade from mountain walls and enough water—even slow seepages are enough—to keep them alive. Each of them grows upward from a great central bud, which the desert Indians occasionally ate after it was roasted. This kills the tree, however; so don't do it! The Indians sometimes burn the dead leaves of the skirt, blackening the trunk, to bring a better crop of the edible fruit. So watch for this sign. They still grind the seeds into a flour to make bread and use the big leaves to thatch a summer hut.

THE TREMBLING ASPENS

We have talked about the remarkable aspens before, but more comment still is needed. All through the mighty mountains of the West, even in the desert ranges of Nevada and Utah, and wherever there is moisture and coolness, the quaking or trembling aspens are the most ubiquitous of trees. They have increased mightily since the coming of the white man, for he has cut and burned out so many of the great coniferous forests that the quaking aspens have come in to fill the void left by the fallen giants. We can be more than thankful to these strange small trees with their ceaselessly talking and dancing leaves, their beautiful white bark, and their leaves that turn to the clearest and most lovely gold in fall, for without them our mountains might indeed turn far more quickly into

Trembling Aspen

Quaking aspen grove near Kamloops, British Columbia.—*Photo courtesy Paul Van Dyke.*

wastelands and deserts under the touch of the spoilers. But the aspen springs up, as under the touch of a sorcerer's wand, on poor and fire-ruined soil, even where the freshets of melting snow or the spring rains have begun to erode the sides of the ridges once protected by the conifers. We should encourage them to grow in more such places, for, around their roots, the soil collects and their falling leaves and rotting branches add to it. Soon they give protection to the seedling trees of the conifers (see Aspens under Nurse Trees in Chapter 4) which will eventually outgrow and kill them. But in the period of transition between the time of man's destruction of the forests and the time of his rebuilding them, the aspens often cover vast areas that might otherwise be barren desert with their forever quivering foliage. And deer, elk, beaver, hares, and rabbits come to feed on their young bark and their leaves when they are low enough, so that aspens support the wildlife of the mountains even when they are helping bring back the greater trees. When you find an aspen cut down, even if by a beaver, count its rings and you will exclaim over how fast it has grown to help hold and build the soil, often twenty-five feet or more in a very few years!

SEMIDESERT WOODLANDS

There are no great deciduous forests in the West to compare to those in the East, with their numerous species and their often dense understories of trees. I remember, as a young man, coming east for the first time, seeing the tall straight eastern oaks and exclaiming that they could not be oaks for they did not fit the picture I had of oaks from the squat, low-spreading trees of California. In the West it is the conifers that reach high to the sky, though the valley oak and the California sycamore are magnificent trees. In the West dryness keeps the size of most of the deciduous trees down; in fact, it turns many of them into dwarfs in the elfin forest of the chaparral.

Oak Woodlands of Oregon, California, Arizona, and New Mexico

Western oaks are generally smaller than eastern oaks and less likely to reach large central trunks toward the heavens, as the eastern oaks are driven to do by the competition of other trees. Western oak woods are divided into the following two major categories you will see as you travel among them.

OPEN OAK GROVES AND SAVANNAS   These are rather exclusively oak areas, with comparatively few other trees. In the great valley of the Willamette River in Oregon, and, to a lesser degree, in large valleys farther north, the massive Oregon oaks make beautiful open groves with grass below, and some scattered Douglas firs, big-leaf maples, and a few other trees present. Similar groves of the still more massive and wide-spreading valley oaks are found in the inland valleys of California, though both kinds of oaks are suffering from the impact of spreading suburbs, which cause many of these grand old monarchs to be cut down. The southeast Arizona and southwest New Mexico mountains and plateaus have some fairly open oak woodlands with the Gambel, Rocky Mountain white, Emory, and Arizona white oaks forming most of the trees (see photo), but with some underbrush of Apache plume, Juneberry, wild plum, chokecherry, skunk brush, and similar bushes.

One of the signs to notice is the distance between different trees in these

Valley Oak

Oregon Oak

Gambel Scrub Oak

Apache Plume

Emory oak grove in Arizona mountains.—*Southern Pacific photo.*

woods. Where far apart there is a dearth of water in the soil; where close together the soil water is greater. The great underground root systems, competing
for the underground water, keep the trees apart. In some parts of California the
oaks are wide enough apart to be called savannas with only scattered oaks here
and there in grasslands. In southern California there are open groves of live
oaks, together with some mesa oaks, with little but grass beneath them. In most
of these oaks the acorns are edible only after being leached thoroughly with
warm water, after which the ground acorns can be baked into bread after grinding, or boiled as mush. But the Rocky Mountain white oak and the Emory oak
furnish sweet acorns that can be eaten straight and have been enjoyed for
generations by the southwest Indians.

Coast Live Oak

FOOTHILL OAK WOODLANDS　　These oaks are generally mixed with
other trees. The oaks in California include live oaks, black oaks, blue oaks, and
golden-cup oaks, with other trees including the Digger pine, the big-cone pine,
the California laurel, buckeye, madrone, and redbud. There is also an understory of such shrubs as the buckbrush, yerba santa, California buckthorn, oak
gooseberry, and poison oak.

Interior Live Oak

The Chaparral

The chaparral (see photo) is a scrub forest, usually created by dry, hot
conditions in summer and fall, that has several divisions in the West. In California, there is the northern coastal scrub, north of San Francisco, in which
coyote brush and various lupines and monkey flowers are the dominant plants;
the coastal sage scrub, from San Francisco south, where California sagebrush,
purple and black sage, lemonade sumach, and California buckwheat brush
dominate; and the true chaparral, in the low interior mountains and foothills,
where chamise, buckthorn, deer brush, toyon, Whipple yucca, also called candle
of the Lord (see Plants That Feed Wildlife in Chapter 5), and California
fremontia are among the many dense, rigid or thorny, small leathery-leaved
plants that cover large areas of dryness. In many parts of Arizona and New

Mesa Oak

Chaparral-covered hills in California.—*Photo courtesy U.S. Forest Service.*

Mountain Mahogany

Apache Plume

Mexico, as well as throughout the lower parts of the southern Rocky Mountains, a similar dwarf woods of thick brush gathers in clumps rather than extensive forests. Scrub oaks, mountain mahogany, sagebrush, and Apache plume are among the dominant plants in such localities.

Many hills and low mountains of California have the chaparral on the dry south-facing slopes and the oak woodlands on the cooler, damper north-facing slopes. The tiny, leathery leaves of the chaparral bushes control transpiration of moisture much better than the leaves of the larger oaks, so the chaparral plants can stand the heat and dryness much better. Because of its denseness and spiny or stiff branches, the true chaparral is probably the least explored part of the Southwest. Hidden under its dense branches are many small wild animal trails and a number of lost mines.

DESERT WOODLANDS

While most of the southwestern deserts of the United States and north-western Mexico are made up of shrubs and smaller plants, here and there fantastic-looking forests appear, created either by yucca trees or the giant saguaro cacti.

The Yucca Forests

Joshua Tree

Yucca plants grow in most of the deserts of the Southwest and as far east as western Texas, but the yucca that creates what looks most like a real forest is the Joshua tree of southeastern California, southern Nevada, Utah, and much of Arizona. Sometimes reaching as high as forty feet, the Joshua tree does so by forking into new branches again and again from below repeating central blooms of large waxy white flowers. Each branch is decorated with clumps of exceedingly sharp-spined, sharp-toothed leaves. The dead leaves of former years create a kind of close-fitting dress about the trunk, where they hang like shingles, usually to the ground. Mormon pioneers, seeing the shaggy and often bearded-looking heads at the ends of branches, imagined strange prophets of the desert, and called them Joshua trees. The spines, of course, as in all desert plants, are meant to discourage animals that, desperately thirsty, would chew at anything that might give a hint of water.

The giant, creamy leather flowers of this yucca have a strange story to tell us. The funguslike smell these flowers send out across the desert in "springtime" (which comes not as do our regular springs, but whenever sufficient moisture falls at a time of neither too much heat or cold) transmits a special message to a special creature. This is the yucca moth (*Tegeticula*), which comes to the flowering yuccas and lays her eggs directly in the plant's ovaries, expecting (however subconsciously) her babies to harvest food from the fruits of the plant when they grow. But the ovules inside the ovaries must be fertilized by pollen, and the yucca moth deliberately makes sure this will happen by carrying pollen to each stigma and placing it directly on it, a unique example of perfect co-operation between a plant and an insect!

Joshua Tree

The fruits of this tree, each looking like a giant ostrich egg, have a further strange adventure. When they drop to the ground on ripening, they begin to tumble and roll before the probing desert wind until their half-capsulelike, half-berrylike covering, with its spongy interior, breaks open and the seeds are shaken out far and wide to start new trees!

Many other animals use the Joshua tree for a home or for food, including the night lizard, which hides under its dead leaves and in its decaying branches and trunks, and the cactus woodpecker, which digs holes in its trunks and branches for nest places, where other birds, like screech owls, wrens, titmice, and bluebirds also find homes in time. Then the Scott's oriole uses the long fibers of the leaves to build splendid hanging nests from the highest branches, while the desert wood rat delights to collect the sharp spines and use them for an impregnable defense of the pile of sticks and other debris from which he makes his nest.

The Saguaro and Cholla Cactus Woodland

Another desert tree, reaching fantastic arms to the sky, is the giant saguaro cactus, sometimes more than thirty or even forty feet tall, spreading spiny forests among the southwest deserts of Arizona. The huge spine-covered branches sometimes dip almost to the ground, carried there by the weight of

Saguaro Cactus

Joshua trees on Mohave Desert.—*Photo courtesy U.S. Forest Service.*

Giant saguaro cacti forest in Arizona.—*Southern Pacific Photo.*

Ocotillo

reserve water held within them, for a saguaro may have within itself as much as four tons of liquid! Naturally, to protect this precious treasure of the desert, the spines outside must be thick and fierce indeed!

With the saguaro are found many other desert plants, including paloverde trees, ocotillo, barrel cactus (whose hidden water has saved the lives of men lost in the desert), and creosote bush, but the most common and also the most dangerous is usually the cholla cactus, of which the largest kind is called the tree cholla. The extraordinarily sharp and back-barbed spines of the cholla are very painful and very difficult to get out once they have penetrated your skin.

Cactus woodpeckers also bore holes in the saguaro, but the most amazing dweller in these holes is the elf owl, whose cute little head can be seen peering out of many a dark hole on moonlit nights. Indians use the large fruits and their seeds for food and drink.

Jumping Cholla

Suggested References

General Books on Forests

McCormick, Jack. *Life of the Forest.* New York: McGraw-Hill Book Co., 1966. (A good general introduction.)

————. *Living Forest.* New York: Harper & Row, 1958.

Neal, Ernest G. *Woodland Ecology.* Cambridge, Mass.: Harvard University Press, 1958.

Spurr, S. H. *Forest Ecology.* New York: The Ronald Press Co., 1964. (Good, but rather technical.)

Watts, May. *Reading the Landscape.* New York: The Macmillan Co., 1966. (An excellent introduction.)

Books on Specific Forests

Braun, E. L. *Deciduous Forests of Eastern North America.* New York: Hafner Publishing Co., 1950.

Steyermark, Julian A. *Vegetational History of the Ozark Forest.* Columbia, Mo.: University of Missouri Press, 1959. (Paperback.)

Forest Fires

Holbrook, Stewart H. *Burning an Empire: The Story of American Forest Fires.* New York: The Macmillan Co., 1943.

Kemp, Larry. *Epitaph for the Giants.* Portland, Oreg.: Touchstone Press, 1967.

Forest Conservation

Brockman, Christian. *Recreational Use of Wild Lands.* New York: McGraw-Hill Book Co., 1959.

Frome, Michael. *Whose Woods These Are: The Story of the National Forests.* Garden City, N.Y.: Doubleday & Co., 1962.

Books on Trees

Baerg, Harry. *How to Know the Western Trees.* Dubuque, Iowa: William C. Brown Co., 1955.

Bowers, Nathan A. *Cone-bearing Trees of the Pacific Coast.* Rev. ed. Palo Alto, Calif.: Pacific Books, 1960.

Coker, William Chambers, and Totten, Henry R. *Trees of the Southeastern States.* Rev. ed. Chapel Hill: University of North Carolina Press, 1945.

Green, Charlotte H. *Trees of the South.* Chapel Hill: University of North Carolina Press, 1939.

Grimm, William Carey. *The Book of Trees.* Harrisburg, Pa.: The Stackpole Co., 1966.

Harolow, William M. *Trees of the Eastern and Central United States and Canada.* New York: Dover Publications, 1942.

Jacques, Harry E. *How to Know the Trees.* Dubuque, Iowa: William C. Brown Co., 1946.

Peattie, Donald C. *Natural History of Trees of Eastern and Central North America.* Boston: Houghton Mifflin Co., 1950. (A very fine feeling in this book for trees.)

——————. *Natural History of Western Trees.* Boston: Houghton Mifflin Co., 1953. (A very fine book.)

Climate and Trees

Geiger, Rudolph. *The Climate near the Ground.* Rev. ed. Cambridge, Mass.: Harvard University Press, 1965. (A fine introduction to microclimates.)

U.S. Department of Agriculture. *Yearbook of Agriculture 1941,* in annual series, "Climate and Man." Washington, D.C.: Government Printing Office, 1941.

Forests and Wildlife

Benton, Allen H., and Werner, William E. *Manual of Field Biology and Ecology.* Minneapolis, Minn.: Burgess Publishing Co., 1965.

Chinery, Michael, and Larkin, D. *Patterns of Living.* Boston: Ginn & Co., 1966.

Dice, Lee R. *Natural Communities.* Ann Arbor: University of Michigan Press, 1952.

Hylander, Clarence J. *Wildlife Community: From the Tundra to the Tropics in North America.* Boston: Houghton Mifflin, 1965.

Shelford, Victor E. *Ecology of North America.* Urbana, Ill.: University of Illinois Press, 1963.

Wild Plants Edible by Humans

Angier, Bradford. *Free for the Eating.* Harrisburg, Pa.: The Stackpole Co., 1966.

——————. *More Free-for-the-Eating Wild Foods.* Harrisburg, Pa.: The Stackpole Co., 1969.

Index